BEING THE
CHANGE
INSPIRED to WIN in
NETWORK MARKETING

Ken Dunn

©Copyright 2011 Evolvlife Publishing

All rights reserved. No part of this book may be reproduced or transmitted in any form or by any means, electronic or mechanical, including photocopying, recording, or by any information storage and retrieval system, without permission in writing from the publisher.

ISBN 978-0-9868368-2-4

Published by EvolvLife Publishing.
1305 Morningside Avenue, Unit 15
Toronto, Ontario, Canada
L1N 2S8

www.evolvlifepublishing.com

www.kendunnleadership.com

Dedication

This book is dedicated to my father, Allen Dunn, who left this life after losing his battle with Lou Gehrig disease at the age of 54. My dad devoted his entire adult life in service to his country. He taught me about commitment and hard work. As I travel the world, I carry his driver's license in my wallet as a constant reminder that he is still with me.

It is because of the lessons I learned from my dad that my family enjoys the freedom we do today.

Acknowledgments

I thank the many people who reached out to me through the years and helped me see that I needed to become a better person. Your efforts did not go in vain.

Most importantly, I thank my best friend, my partner and my love, Julie. Thank you so much for always encouraging me and for sticking with me and supporting me, even in the darkest hours. *Love, Laughter and Friendship...*

To my beautiful kids, Matthew and Laura: I love you both so much. You make me smile and laugh. Everything I do in my life is for you.

To my dear friends Juan Carlos and Hortensia Barrios, you have been such a blessing to my life.

Finally, to all of you who believe that change is possible: THANK YOU!

Table of Contents

Foreword

I first met Ken Dunn—not in person, which I'm eagerly looking forward to—when I was hunting & gathering people for my book, *The Greatest Networkers in the World— 21 ordinary people who became millionaires in Network Marketing and the true stories of how they did it.* I knew that Ken was one of a select group of industry leaders who were presenters at Art Jonak's MasterMind Events. So, I began to do my research into who and how he was, both as a Network Marketer and a human being.

The more I learned about Ken, the more I knew he had to be in the book.

Ken Dunn IS one of The Greatest Networkers in the World.

There was a formula we used back at the old Success magazine when selecting successful entrepreneurs to do feature articles about. They had to have a "dog food moment." It went like this: They had their great success and were flying high. Then, they lost it all to the point where they were at rock bottom and eating dog food from a can. But they picked themselves up, started over, and made it back on top.

In *Being the Change...* you'll learn all about Ken's "dog food moment," and he will show you and tell you precisely what he did to get back on top. It's a remarkable journey.

There are "How to" books and "Why to" books, but this book is neither of those— although it's filled with powerful and persuasive how and why to do those things that create real and lasting success. *Being the Change...* is different. It's a "Who to" book. It's about who to BECOME and BE to win in Network Marketing and keep on winning.

There a famous saying: "Give a man a fish and you've feed him for a day. Teach a man to fish and you've fed him for a lifetime." With Ken in mind I'll add another line: "Teach a man to teach other men to fish and you'll feed the world."

There's a requirement I have for books I read & write: They must inform, involve & inspire. *Being the Change...* does that, and more. I know you'll enjoy it.

Thanks.

I appreciate you.

John Milton Fogg

Introduction

Through a series of events—known as 2x4s up the side of the head—I realized how terrible my outlook on life was, how flawed I had become, and how terribly I treated other people. Once my faults were thrown out into the open for all to see—especially me—I set a course to give myself a whole new and improved personality. And I was blessed to know from the beginning that skin deep wouldn't cut it. No redecorating or retrofitting. I had to completely redesign and then rebuild myself from the inside out.

My goal in life had always been to create wealth for my family and I'd done very well at that: Four multi-million dollar businesses in different industries in less than six years. Not bad.

But no real and lasting friendships! Partnerships based on win-win, as long as I won more. Close, caring relationships I could count on one hand – my wife and kids. Not good.

I realized I had to become a better person.

This book is not just another of those personal development sagas with the hidden agenda of furthering a career. Nor was it written to inflate my ego or increase my reputation— what I have to say just might do more damage to my name in the short run.

I wrote *Being the Change,* because I am choosing to be accountable for my own greatness and to help you develop yours.

During the past five years, I've had to totally change who I am. I decided to publish my story and the facts to set the broken records straight and to share my best discoveries with you to launch both of us into a powerful new future of personal and professional success.

In this book, you will learn how I personally received guidance and mentoring from some of the world's elite leaders: Bill Gates, Warren Buffett, Steve Jobs, Mahatma Gandhi, Mother Teresa, John F. Kennedy, and Pierre Trudeau. They showed me through their examples the incredible possibilities for my life.

As I rolled up my sleeves and dug down into the hard work (and it really is *hard work*) of becoming a better person, I was continually encouraged to dig deeper and reach higher by the results I was getting— and I started getting more positive outcomes right away! The moment that I started working on me, my entire life became better, our family income increased, the number and quality of my relationships expanded, my circle of friends got bigger and bigger— and better and better— and my partnerships became stronger and I played together with my partners at a much higher level.

The road to becoming a better person— and ultimately becoming a leader— has been a long, pretty bumpy and often painful one.

But at the same time, it's been the most exhilarating and rewarding journey of my life.

I am not the inspiration to others that I hope to be... YET! Publishing this book literally inspires me to continue on the journey to becoming a better person. To ramp it up and play for even more. Yet, there's another, much deeper reason that I have decided to publish this book.

Over the past five years, I have traveled all over the world and met thousands of people. In my travels, I've encountered many people who had a burning desire to create success, people who desperately wanted to change their lives for the better. Because of my own experience and efforts working on myself, once I got to know these people I was able to easily identify those aspects of their personality that were holding them back from achieving that success.

Every one of us has personal habits and traits that don't serve us. Whether it's constantly interrupting others because we aren't really listening... or talking too much because we're rambling on and on and on about our opinions and ourselves... having to be right... not truly caring about others... not telling the truth no matter what... *Being the Change* will help you to take a closer look at your own life, determine what personal traits and habits you have that could potentially be holding you back, and learn how to shift them for the better.

My hope is that as you read this book and learn about all of the challenges I've had with my personality you will realize some of your own limitations (and ways to make a change) through me and mine.

I'll show you how those little issues, subtle faults and flaws, could actually be the *biggest* reason for your lack of success.

Finally, I know that as you read this book, you'll likely think of someone that's facing the same challenges I've gone through. It can be pretty difficult to point out to other people areas where they need to improve themselves. Most people are caring folks and don't want to offend others.

We also have this "don't want to get involved in other people's stuff" mindset, so we avoid pointing out where someone else might need to make improvements in their personality.

So when you're reading the book, when my story makes you think of a friend who may have some of those similar challenges in their personality, **GIVE THEM THIS BOOK!**

How It All Started

Before starting my first Network Marketing business, I was a cop, a career police detective investigating drug dealers, robberies, rapes and murders. At the same time, I was running my own successful mortgage company with nine full-time employees and hundreds of millions of dollars in revenue. I joined the Network Marketing profession in 2003 at the urging of a good friend.

In my first year in the business, I earned more than eighty thousand dollars.

Now, you may think that's all a great success story: 15 years on the force, million-dollar business, one of the rare take-off-like-a-rocket starts in Network Marketing. Okay, it IS impressive, BUT... there's a down-side to the story.

In my first year in Network Marketing I built my business with a police detective's mindset and personality. That's what made me so successful so fast. And that's what made me UNsuccessful just as fast, too.

I'd been a cop my entire adult life. I had developed a very dark and jaded view of people. Combine that with a self-centered personality (code for "an ego that was committed to being right, because *being right was my job"*). I was controlling and dictatorial in my interactions and behavior with people.

And as you might guess, I built my Network Marketing business with that same personality. Hey, if it's not broke don't fix it— right?

Wrong. Very wrong.

Fueled by an equally dictating, controlling, self-centered, first mentor in the business— whose ego was even more out of control than mine— I became one of the least liked leaders in my company.

I built the business using the same methods as my mentor: Fear, Intimidation, and Control.

At the end of my first year in the business, my two best leaders quit. Now, when your two biggest leaders quit your business, 90% of your business goes away with them, and that's exactly what happened to me! Virtually overnight my income went from a consistently growing $25,000 a month to $2,000.

The first couple of days after they quit were the most painful days of my life. I cried (and cops *do not cry*). I withdrew into my own world— a world of despair. I never felt so lost. So alone.

As I emerged out of the haze of beating myself up and self-pity, I realized there was only one thing I could do— change. Big time.

I had to become a better person...

I HAD TO!

I went to these two ex-leaders of mine— and a number of the other "most important people" in my life— and asked each one of them to point out everything wrong in my personality... all my shortcomings... every place I fell short and HAD to improve.

They ended up giving me a list of *40 things* I had to change! (Who knew?)

I was prepared for 10 or 12... maybe. That was way more than enough. But *40* ... I didn't know anyone could have *40 things wrong with them!*

What a painful experience that was!

Wow!

A short time later, through an innocent Easter gift from my wife Julie, which I'll tell you about later in the book, I was compelled to study seven of the world's most inspirational and influential leaders. As I drilled-down into the lives and achievements of these seven remarkable men and women who truly changed the world, I watched in amazement as 10 common characteristics emerged.

I realized that if I just focused on these 10 characteristics *in myself,* my entire life would be transformed.

I was right. It has been!

As you read *Being the Change,* you will learn the *10 traits inspirational leaders embody.* You'll also gain the knowledge and skill to apply these characteristics in your life and work and FINALLY achieve the success you are seeking.

You will clearly see how each of these icons of our world identified the *core task* in their life and then focused all their passion and energy on accomplishing that *core task.* You will also learn in the chapters of this book that the *core task* in Network Marketing— and yes it is everyone's *core task*— is *prospecting.* You will know what to do to have prospecting be natural and automatic. And when you do, the lifestyle you're looking for will be yours naturally and automatically as well.

One of the biggest things I've realized during my journey in Network Marketing is that there is too much emphasis on personal growth and development *too soon*. Before you get sucked into that abyss, you have to get good at prospecting.

I know, I know. It seems like I'm sticking the horse in the back of the cart. Look, what you'll learn by getting good at prospecting IS pretty much all the personal growth you'll ever need. And "earn while you learn" is a much better deal than investing a small fortune and all that time in books, CDs and seminars you can't afford yet.

Please, don't get me wrong.

Personal growth IS where it's at in this business. My point is: "When it's at," is just as important.

In this book, you will learn the secrets to second nature recruiting. You will watch how I've created an endless "living list of leads," and you'll learn why follow-up is truly NOT as important as many leaders and trainers make it.

Now, what could you achieve if you had a list of 10 traits to focus on for the rest of your life?

If you commit to focusing on these traits, then I promise you will achieve the success that's eluded you.

How can I promise you that? Because I did it! I know it's possible and I know HOW to do it. This book will teach you that— and more.

As you read through the chapters of this book, you'll learn how to create your own *gravitational pull*. When you walk into a room, your presence will captivate everyone. You will finally understand why it is so important to create a more likeable personality and precisely how to do it.

You will learn why *mentorship* is so important, and you'll learn how to pick the right mentor for you— and perhaps even more important, what to do to avoid the wrong ones. If you don't know what to watch for some "mentors" could ruin your life. (It nearly happened to me).

As you read *Being the Change* and learn about the things I have been through on my road to a seven-figure annual Network Marketing income, think about your own journey and apply those same traits to your life. You will finally understand why personal development is so important, when and how to employ it for best advantage and how to develop yourself without defocusing on the core task.

I am absolutely convinced that when you apply the 10 characteristics of inspirational leadership to your life and work, you will create the lifestyle that you desire, dream of and deserve.

1

My Journey

Like many others, my journeys in entrepreneurship are "rags to riches" stories, beginning when I was a child in Halifax, Nova Scotia. I've always been the ultimate dreamer, even though I was the oldest of three children growing up in a pretty poor environment with my younger brother and sister. Our dad worked for the Canadian Navy his entire life and although he did the best he could, working for the Navy didn't pay him very well.

At a very early age I knew exactly what it felt like to be broke, so I know what it feels like for many families today who are stuck in that same place. I guess you could say I came from fairly humble beginnings. I say that.

I mean, a weekly highlight for us was having fried baloney for dinner on Wednesday night!

Our family was so poor that my folks couldn't afford to buy clothes for all of us, so we took advantage of the Salvation Army. I was so embarrassed when the other kids ridiculed and made fun of me for wearing shabby hand-me-downs that by the time I was 12 years old I began stealing clothes.

I would wear sneakers until I had literally worn holes through the bottoms of them. This was back when all the kids were wearing Converse basketball shoes. Remember those red-and-white high tops? Those were the days of Dr. J and everyone was wearing them, except me.

As a dreamer, I was always looking for ways to change my present situation. So, I created an "exchange program" where I would actually walk into the department store wearing my old worn-out sneakers, try on a new pair, and then just walk right out wearing the new shoes as if they were mine.

One day I walked into the department store, tried on a pair of new high tops and then walked out with them on leaving my old ones behind. As I was leaving, this big guy came up and grabbed me by the arm and said, "I'm with store security. I need you to come with me." I saw my life flash before my eyes. I knew that when my dad found out life as I knew it was going to be over. I was scared to death.

The security officer pulled me back into the office and sat me down. He started to interrogate me and said, "I know you stole those watches. What did you do with them?"

He had no idea that I was sitting there wearing the department store's sneakers. He thought I had stolen something else and was so focused on that he didn't notice.

I adamantly denied stealing the watches. I was sweating bullets the whole time. Then my dad— a very stern military man— showed up. The security officer began to tell him what had happened. Finally, when the security guy realized I had nothing to do with stealing watches, my dad and I were free to go. We walked out of the store with me wearing the new sneakers from my "exchange program."

That moment changed my life. For many children that get away with stealing things at a young age, it's the beginning of a career in crime. I spent 15 years in police work where I saw that happen for many kids. Minor theft was where it all started. Their lives in crime progressed from there.

But I was different.

That day I decided that I needed more and wanted better in my life and that I was going to do something honest to earn those things.

I never wanted to feel like that again. I knew I couldn't steal anymore.

I'm not proud of this part of my history. The reason I'm mentioning it is to give you an idea of the pain from my past that fuels my "Why" and drives me today.

The Disease of Entrepreneurialism

When I was 16 I got a job working in a service station, pumping gas. About a year later, I overheard the owner talking about needing to buy a tow truck, but how he didn't want to go through the hassles of managing it. So, Ken the Dreamer convinced him to let me drive the tow truck and I'd manage it.

I began driving the truck every day to school. I used to skip classes to tow cars. I carried one of those big old, clunky, black, the-size-of-a-Blackberry pagers. Remember them? They used to go off with an annoying *beep-beep-beep-beep*. My pager would go off in right the middle of physics class and I'd get up and leave to tow a car.

That first year driving that tow truck around part-time, I earned more money than my dad did! I was able to contribute to the family and add some ease to our lifestyle. That's when the "disease of entrepreneurialism" first appeared in my life. I've been "cursed" with it since. And in my case, there is no cure.

I've always dreamed of a better life. That's my "Why."

In Network Marketing we're always told that we need to have a strong "Why." We're going to talk a lot about what leads and drives people, and the importance of having a strong reason "Why" later on in this book. The thoughts that I've just described are the ones that motivate me every day of my life; they are my "Why."

My deepest desire is that none of my descendants go through the same experiences of poverty and pain that I did.

There have been many books written and many studies done that suggest that for the most part, generation after generation people remain the same.

I remember in law enforcement, you could go back 10 generations of fathers and sons, and they were all cops. Or a son becomes a certified public accountant because that's what his dad did. Mothers, daughters and their daughters in the same family were nurses or doctors. Statistics show that more often than not, you will become what your father or mother was.

Joel Osteen's book, *Becoming a Better You*, had a big impact on me. He said that even though that's the way it is, people have the ability to break the cycle by deciding to take action, to stop whatever that recurring generational pattern is and move forward.

In my family the recurring pattern had been poverty. It wasn't just my dad. My grandfather was a plumber and battled with money his whole life. He and my dad had bad lines of credit and were in debt over their heads.

Years before I read Osteen's book, I decided that I was going to break the cycle of poverty in my family.

That's why I drove the tow truck through the rest of high school. Now obviously, driving that truck every day meant that I managed to miss most of my classes. I barely graduated and I really had no interest in pursuing any further education.

I wanted to make more money, but I didn't know what kind of job I could get to make the kind of money I wanted. I didn't have a dollar sign in mind. There was just no way I was going to live like I had when I was younger.

When it comes to success, I don't think age matters at all. In fact, I hesitate to tell people how old I am because there's always a stigma as soon as they learn my age. Many people have a hard time believing that somebody can really achieve multiple seven-figure income results before they're 40.

I want this book to be the proof that I've been through as much, if not more, struggle and suffering as anybody else. I just decided to expedite my exit from the pain game, *and so can YOU!*

Luckily, through this entire ten-year process, I've made notes, I've had recollections, and I've been able to put it all into a process. I've identified a success track for people to truly become wealthy, regardless of their backgrounds.

My Career in Law Enforcement

I knew I didn't want to drive a tow truck for the rest of my life, but I didn't have a clue about what I could do instead.

I certainly was not the most scholarly guy in high school. I was definitely never expected to be successful in my life. I still have my high school yearbooks, and a couple of my buddies wrote in the back of one of them,

"Most likely to end up in jail."

You never know where life is going to take you. Look back through your own high school days. Isn't it funny how the people we expected to be doctors and lawyers are blue-collar workers, and those we expected to fail are successful? Maybe desire truly can make dreams come true…

At the end of my senior year, the school held a career day. We were all forced to attend. The Halifax police had a booth there; they were recruiting. I started asking them questions, and they said, "Well, you have to be 21." They told me to check back in a couple of years.

Now, right next to the police was a booth for the Canadian Armed Forces, and the recruiter overheard me talking to the Halifax police officer, because as I walked past he said,

"Would you think about the military police?"

I had no idea what or who they were.

The long and short of it was I ended up joining the Canadian military when I was 18 years old, and I became a police officer. Coming right out of basic training I went into investigation work. I spent my first couple of years in law enforcement investigating Canada's significant drug trafficking problem. I did a lot of undercover work in those first two years.

I moved to another city in Canada and spent the next three years working in a local police department with a SWAT team in tactical policing. We did all kinds of special operations like armed ship boarding, drug entry— really amazing things.

During this time, I met my wife Julie. She's my inspiration and my best friend. She's managed to put up with me, stick with me, motivate and inspire me through all these years.

Julie was finishing her nursing degree and we hit it off right away. We fell in love, spent hours and hours talking on the phone and then she moved with me to Charlottetown, Prince Edward Island, where I was policing at the time. We stayed there together for a couple of years and then ended up moving to Ottawa where I became a police officer with the Ottawa police service.

During this whole time I was involved in a number of entrepreneurial things.

A Baby Changes Everything!

Things really changed for me when I turned 30. Julie and I had a beautiful house on four acres in Ottawa and a pile of debt to go with it. My son was born on July 15, 2001. Your life changes instantly the minute you see your first child. It is such an incredible, humbling experience. The first thing I thought as I stared at my newborn boy was,

"You're going to have a better life than me. I am going to make that happen!"

Prior to my son being born, I thought I was bulletproof. In my first 10 years in law enforcement, I did a lot of undercover drug work. I was on a SWAT team and I saw many, many people die.

During this time, nothing ever bothered me. I was never worried about my own safety. But the minute my son was born… I realized I wasn't some superhero. I was a human being— I bled and I could die. I ended up taking life a whole lot more seriously, literally overnight.

At that time, I was investigating a murder. I observed the devastation of that family's loss. I attended the funeral of the man who was murdered, and looking at his two-year-old son, I just couldn't stop crying.

It was amazing how my entire emotional state changed as a result of Matthew coming into my life. If you're a parent, you know what I mean. I began to realize that it was time for me to get out of police work. I was 30 years old. I didn't want to be a cop anymore.

In Canada, police officers are paid very well, especially detectives because they are paid for an amazing amount of overtime. I was making over $100,000 a year, but I was spending $120,000 a year. We had a $400,000 home with a $225,000 mortgage, two brand-new cars (both leased), and over $125,000 in maxed out credit cards.

I'd get paid on Friday and by Tuesday I'd be broke again.

I don't know how the heck it happened, but history *was* repeating itself. I *was* my father's son. Does this sound familiar to you? It's incredible how many people in North America are living the same way.

I remember managing to pay six credit cards and the lines of credit making the minimum payments on them. But as soon as I got the minimum payment on one line of credit, I'd take it on again to pay the other credit card. Or, I'd pay as much as I could and then go into an interview with the police credit union and get one of the lines of credit increased so I could make my car payments.

I mean, how pathetic was Christmas for me? I know it is possible that some of you might stop reading the book when you read this sentence, because you're living this right now. You know, you get through Christmas and you've accumulated all that credit card debt. Everything you buy is on credit cards. Then you spend the next six months trying to pay them off.

This was the life I was living. I realized when my son was born that I hated my job and I wanted a change. Okay, I didn't *really* hate my job— I loved the work. I just wanted more and better. I was sick of the environment that I was in, and I was tired of making great money and being broke.

So, I did what many typical Americans do when they realize they hate their job and want something more...

I went out to look for *another* job.

I didn't have any experience or education outside of law enforcement— and $100,000 is a lot of money to replace. I guarantee that some of you will have a tear in your eye when you read this, because you're in that same sinking boat right now. I've found out since that this is the way *most* Canadians and Americans live.

The best thing I found was running security at the hospital for $40,000 a year. How would I ever make ends meet?

I remember sitting on the corner of my bed one night. Julie was asleep. My little son, Matthew, was asleep. I sat on the bed and cried. I had no idea what I was going to do. Absolutely none. I wanted so desperately to have a better life, to create a better life for my family, but I felt completely lost and alone.

New Opportunities

When I first moved to Ottawa, my wife and I lived in a condominium, and we paid condo fees. We had to pay $300 a month in our condo for our contribution to the grounds maintenance, etcetera. We were in a 17-unit building. It drove me crazy because there was very little actually being done.

I went to the condominium corporation and said, "Pay me the money, and I'll take care of all of the renovations. Cut the grass. Everything."

Then an idea popped into my entrepreneurial head: I'll get a couple more of these condos and start doing the same thing for more people and make more money."

Luckily, in law enforcement I worked a schedule that consisted of four days on, four days off. This allowed me plenty of time to start a part-time business. I could manage that. So, I went out and pitched myself to a couple more condominium corporation boards and ended up having three different condominiums to take care of with almost 80 units. I was making about $15,000 a month in the beginning.

The Best Education Is Practical Experience

What started off as a great idea to create extra money on the side eventually became a nightmare, because I got so busy that I had to hire somebody else to do the snowplowing, cut the grass and hire a handyman to do the maintenance in the buildings while I was managing the entire operation.

I was bringing in $15,000 in revenue monthly, but by the time everybody else got paid I made $500 a month. And I was working my tail off.

My solution was to sell that business and I made some really great money when I did. This was an amazing learning

22

experience in hiring people to do the work and learning how to leverage my time and energy. I knew that it wasn't working properly, but learning about leverage was a really valuable.

So, I was struggling along. I started to open a few really neat businesses. I realized that if I was going to fix my problems with money, I couldn't find a job that would pay me enough, so the answer had to be working for myself.

Why would I want to spend all my time making someone else rich?

I had no idea what it was like to open a business. I had no idea about the owner being the last one to get paid and all that stuff. But I had it set in my mind that I'd have to open some type of business to make my fortune.

A couple of months later, a friend of mine came back from Mexico. While he was there, he found out how inexpensive sterling silver is if you buy it from the source. I went back to Mexico with him and we visited a city called Taxco (sounds like "tasco"), the place where all the sterling silver jewelry is actually made. Big, bulky silver chains that sold for hundreds of dollars in the U.S. and Canada could be purchased directly from the manufacturer in Mexico for $5.00 to $10.00 dollars. We saw the business idea right away.

We came back to Canada, got an importer's license, and started importing and selling the jewelry. Within a year, we had brought more than $2 million of sterling silver jewelry into Canada. We were making incredible money. I was making four times more money in this business than I had in law enforcement and I was beginning to get some of my debt under control.

It was a great business, but again, I was working like crazy. (And I was still working full-time in law enforcement). I was also a bit nervous because of potential issues with NAFTA (North American Free Trade Agreement). I decided to sell my share of the business, which ended up being another profitable decision for me.

The Course Is Set...

A few months later, in 2002, right around Christmas, my personal banker paid me a visit at home in Ottawa. She saw how successful I was with my silver business and came to me with a proposal. Sabah had gotten into the mortgage industry and was a regional sales manager for a mortgage company.

We were good friends, but on this visit, she came over with a couple of beautiful pictures for our house, presents for the kids, and some really great cards for me, more than she'd ever done before.

I knew she wanted something, but I wasn't sure what.

Eventually she asked me what I thought about getting into the mortgage industry. I told her I couldn't leave my job and she said, "No, I just want you to start part-time."

We started joking around about it and our joking got almost confrontational in a fun way. I was 31 years old, very cocky, and when she told me the types of incomes that the top guys were making I said, "If I do this, I'll be the top guy in this mortgage company in my first two years."

In 2002, the mortgage market was on fire. Interest rates had just dropped and I had a remarkable database to work with: 1,000 police officers who all trusted me.

I've realized that one of the most important virtues in life and business is trust and I had the perfect example in this situation. I sent out an inter-office email to everybody announcing that I was now able to arrange mortgages for them.

In my first month in the mortgage industry, I earned about $18,000— and this was doing it very part-time. By the end of the first year, I had to hire an assistant to process all the paperwork. We actually funded over $25 million in mortgages and my family made just over $300,000. And again, this was part-time. Unbelievable!

The business kept ramping up. In the second year, I hired four full-time brokers to work for me and my income doubled.

In 2003 I became the top broker in my province (state). My company funded around $40 million in mortgages. Things were going great.

My Introduction to Network Marketing

In September 2003, Network Marketing entered the picture.

Julie and I decided that at the end of 2003, if everything kept going the same way with my mortgage business, I would quit my job at the police department. All of my debt had been paid off and things were going very well.

A friend of mine got involved in a Network Marketing business selling nutritional supplements, He wanted me to get involved, too. I told him he was absolutely crazy.

There was no way in the world I was ever going to get involved in MLM, Network Marketing, direct sales, or whatever you called it.

Back in 1999, while I was still a police officer, I worked in a fraud investigation where we investigated a number of pyramid schemes. During our investigation, we studied Network Marketing companies. We had to be able to testify in court differentiating between what was legal and what was illegal.

I had the chance to attend some legitimate Network Marketing company meetings. We sat in the back of the room and listened to the speakers and watched what they were doing and how they were acting. I remember leaning over to my partner, laughing and said, "If I ever join one of these Network Marketing things, just shoot me." That summed up my attitude towards Network Marketing.

I was a really arrogant police officer. I thought all Network Marketers were loony. I thought it was all just absolutely silly. These people would stand up in front of a room and tell people, "If you follow your dreams and float on air you can become rich." I thought they were totally out to lunch.

They were trying to be these perfect people; caring more about others than themselves. I just couldn't believe that stuff. I knew how hard I was working in my conventional businesses, plus I was there with a very skeptical mindset, because I had to understand what it was all about so that I could testify in court what was legal and what was not.

Once I was at a Mary Kay meeting, sitting in the back row, and I couldn't believe this woman up on stage. She was a National Sales Director.

There was a pink Cadillac right in the middle of this meeting room and there were about 200 people in the audience. Throughout the whole presentation I felt like she was staring at me. We were just there to check the business model out and make a few notes, but I could feel her looking directly at me the entire time. Just joking around, I leaned over to my buddy and said, "I think she's after me. She's going to make me join this thing."

The presentation ended and I noticed my partner had disappeared. Now, at these big presentations, what typically happens is that the speaker gets down off the stage, there's lots of handshaking, a few pictures taken and maybe an autograph or two. Well, in this case, the speaker made a beeline right to the back of the room, heading straight for me.

She grabbed my hand and said...

> *"I don't know who you are, but your being here is a testament to how badly you want to make changes in your life. I'd like to make you one of the first men to drive a pink Cadillac."*

I couldn't believe it! Needless to say, the offer to drive that pink Cadillac confirmed my negative opinion of Network Marketing. Pink Cadillac indeed!

So when my friend approached me about Network Marketing, that was the furthest idea from my mind. I was totally focused on my mortgage business. My friend was in real estate at the time and didn't think I would be interested, so he waited for several months before he invited me to take a look at the business.

Interestingly, he referred all of his clients to me and I was making over $100,000 a month from his referrals. You can bet that when he finally did ask me to take a look at his business, there was no way I could say no.

He introduced me to his upline who was my friend's coach and had introduced him to the business. I went to a meeting where there were six guys, all of them with big checks showing off all the money they had made, and my friend's upline was the guy up front drawing the lines and circles on the board.

I had no interest in being there. It was just a big joke to me.

While this gentleman was drawing diagrams I was answering phone calls, dialing numbers, and walking away during his presentation, but he stayed patient the entire time. I walked out of the meeting and I didn't really have a clue what it was all about.

Two days later, my friend asked me to join and I agreed, even though I had no real interest, I was intrigued and I really liked my friend. And as I said, that $100,000 of income every month was very persuasive.

I was busier than you could possibly imagine. I was investigating a murder at the time. On the side, I was running a mortgage company with nine full-time employees, doing hundreds of millions of dollars in sales. And then Network Marketing comes along.

In Network Marketing we talk about systems and how to do the business. But I've always been an independent thinker. If I get a thought in my mind, I do it— and I do it my way. That has sometimes cost me a lot, but it's also made me some great money. I enjoy being an independent thinker.

When Network Marketing came along, I wasn't sure if I was going to take it seriously. Since my friend really wanted me to get involved, I'd just call up my buddies and say…

"Hey, I found a business opportunity. My friend got me involved. It's a Network Marketing company. I don't really care if you join or not, but I want you to sit down with my friend and hear about it so he'll leave me alone."

Powerful, don't you think?

The guys that I talked to sat down with my friend and he explained the business to them; most of the time I wasn't even there. Yet out of the eight guys I talked to in the first month, seven of them joined the business. I was blown away! And … I had no idea what I was into yet. I started to take the business seriously when I got a check for $2,800 after the first month. I couldn't believe how little effort I put into making that kind of money.

Now it all started to make sense. I had flashbacks to those seminars I sat through when I was a cop and what that Mary Kay lady said on stage. I started to study the business model. In my fourth month, my wife and I earned over $10,000 and I quit my job at the police department. My buddies at work all made fun of me, and some of them still do to this day.

Whenever I had an idea, I would always look for somebody who was ultimately successful in that field, whether it was the mortgage business, importing, or property management, and I'd get them to give me some advice on what they did to become successful. Then I'd just do what they told me. I looked for someone like that in Network Marketing right away too.

I was very, very lucky, because my local upline happened to be a guy who was making $100,000 a month in Network Marketing.

Advice from the Top

We continued to build the business. After about five months I had made $25,000. The upline guy who was making $100,000 a month invited me to a generic training in Houston, Texas. At this event, I met leaders from all over the industry— people like Art Jonak, Mark Yarnell, Tom "Big Al" Schreiter, Richard Brooke, Michael Clouse, Eric Worre, Randy Gage and Paula Pritchard— and I was amazed by all of them.

I spoke to several people at that event that were all making ridiculous money. I told each of them the same thing: That I wanted to earn $100,000 a month. I want to become a millionaire in Network Marketing. And I asked them for advice on how to make it happen?

They gave me two very simple, very powerful pieces of advice:

Our business is about introducing the opportunity to new people. Never stop introducing it to new people.

You must grow as a person. You must develop yourself.

"This is a personal development business," they all told me. "Be somebody who's always learning. Read lots of books and do everything you can to develop and grow who you are."

40 Situations to Change

Now everything was going great— or so I thought.

One day over the Christmas holidays that year, two of my top reps came over to my house. I thought they were bringing gifts, but they were empty handed. I invited them in, but they told me they just had something to tell me and said, "We quit."

I was floored! Shell shocked. I couldn't believe what I heard. These guys were making good money, too.

And what was their reason for quitting?

Me!

They went on to tell me that the man who was mentoring me was an outright villain. He was just in it for the money, and they felt I was developing the same personality.

They walked away... and so did about 90% of my downline.

I'll be really honest with you; I cried for a couple days. It was a very humiliating and humbling experience to have somebody lay it all out in front of you like that, telling you what a terrible person you were.

Those guys pointed out some really serious flaws in my character. They told me that I was becoming a dictator. Thing is, I quickly began to see they were right.

I was the guy who'd look people straight in the face and say, "The reason you're failing is because you're no good at this." I'd tell them to quit.

I had fallen head over heels in love with Network Marketing, but I realized that if I was going to be successful, it would require big changes on my part.

The only thing my friends didn't tell me was *how* to make those changes.

I have since learned a lot about what good mentoring is, which I'll cover later in a separate chapter on that topic. But what I started to realize about this mentor of mine was that my friends were correct. He *was* an absolute villain.

He never allowed me to be an independent thinker. And remember, this is a volunteer army we have here. Nobody *has to* do anything. But he would berate and belittle me on the phone, calling me up with one of his top guys on the line with him and criticize me to the point that I was almost in tears. Why? Because I went off and tried some things on my own and he didn't like that.

"My way or hit the highway."

This was my first year of Network Marketing and— even though I been a tough cop for 15 years— this was my first encounter with someone like this.

But the worst part of it was… I *was* becoming more and more like him.

Throughout my whole life, I've always found a mentor that had the success that I want and followed them. I've taken whatever they've done and tried to do it even better.

But this was my first mentor in Network Marketing and I'd picked the wrong one. It was an unbelievable experience.

Because I recognized that I had to change, I decided to talk to two men that had known me for more than five years… two people that had known me for less than five years… and I talked to my cousin who I admired and trusted completely. I told them all…

"Hey, here's what happened. I'm looking for some direction from you. I have no idea what to do. I want you to take the gloves off and tell me what requires

**improvement in my life, because I really
need some assistance with this."**

This is still difficult for me to talk about even many years later.

These people each gave me several areas that required improvement. I ended up with a list of *forty* things that were wrong with me and needed to be fixed. Wow!

Talk about eating humble pie! I served myself up about six pies in one sitting. And it was humiliating, but at least now I knew the things that I had to change. However, I had no direction. I had nobody to work with.

I believe that everything happens in life for a reason and I also believe that good things do come to good people. There's a book I read a while ago by Stephen Post and Jill Neimark called *Why Good Things Happen to Good People*, and I believe that's true.

I was trying to figure out how to do Network Marketing the right way. I had this long list of things that I knew I needed to improve upon. Now was the time for change. So, I apologized to as many people as I could that were in business with me that first year.

One thing Network Marketing taught me is that every day is a new day. You have a chance to start over again every day that you're in this business.

So, these were new days for me and I was intent on starting over.

A List of Forty Points to Improvement

As I mentioned, I asked several people to honestly share those areas in me they felt required improvement. I began by speaking with two people that had known me for more than five years.

Here's what they told me:

The first person:

- Arrogant
- Egotistical
- Self-centered
- Argumentative
- Controlling
- Ignorant
- Didn't care about other people

The second person:

- Self-serving
- Demanding
- Too aggressive with others
- Used foul language
- Abrasive
- Condescending

Then, I talked to two people that knew me for less than five years:

The first person:

- Didn't care about others
- Money-focused

- Moody
- Belligerent
- Control freak
- Dictator
- Greedy
- Bad personality
- Self-serving
- Pushes too hard

The second person:

- Talks too much
- Puts others down
- Argues too much with others
- Always points out others' weaknesses
- Loses patience too fast
- Needs to be more relaxed
- Too uptight
- Too controlling

And my cousin:

- Too tenacious
- Too aggressive
- Too hard on people
- Arrogant
- Money-hungry

- Decisions are all about myself

- Greedy

- Self-centered

- Belligerent

- Pushes others too much

- Doesn't care about anyone else

Every Day Is a Fresh Start

Another rep of mine lived in Mexico. He asked me to do a three-way call with a man in Mexico named Juan Carlos Barrios. Juan Carlos had built a Diamond distributorship in one of the biggest Network Marketing companies in the world. He's an amazing leader, and in fact, he built his Diamond distributorship during the very year that the Mexican currency was devalued. He created a massive residual income in spite of a very tough comp plan, making over $50,000 a month at the height of his career with this company. He was making millions of dollars in his business.

My partner had arranged for me to speak to Juan Carlos on the phone about expanding our business in Mexico. Because they were friends, Juan Carlos Barrios joined our business, but he never did anything. I flew down to Mexico City about a month later to meet with Juan Carlos and my friend.

When I met Juan, I met a human being that was unlike anybody I've ever met in my life.

He's one of the most open, friendly, pleasant people I've ever encountered. We talked for hours and hours.

We talked about where we came from, all the similarities in our lives, and on and on. I forgot all about the business.

During a four-hour conversation, I never told him about our business at all, or the money I'd made.

We ended up building a really significant friendship in the coming months and years, and it all started from that one conversation. After that meeting, Juan Carlos came into the industry again and went back to work. Within six months he had built the largest downline in our company in Mexico. I was flying back and forth to Mexico every month to work with him. This was the kind of mentor that I was looking for.

What you'll find is that mentors will come into your life at times and in ways that you don't expect. I realized that I didn't know how to love people. I never told Juan Carlos this, but he was all about love, and he built very strong allegiances in his groups.

He taught me how to openly love and express myself to others, how to show them that I really do care about them, and how to praise people and build the business through passion.

I had this humiliating experience and I had these forty points to work on, and in a seemingly unconnected way, Juan Carlos comes along and begins teaching me about people and how to be a better person.

Even though he was in my downline and I was his upline, he was always praising me and telling me what a great person I was. I observed how he interacted with people and how everybody loved him. He's just an amazing human being. He's built a big business, we built an incredible friendship, and along the way he taught me what love is all about.

Then, on Easter in 2005, my wife Julie (who I can never say enough about— and when she reads this I want it to be another way for me to express to her how much I love her and owe her for sticking with me through all these difficult experiences) gave me a stencil— a little saying on a piece of plastic with a Popsicle-stick-like thing to rub it onto the wall.

The words are from Gandhi. I'm looking at it right now as I write this. I look at it at least 10 times every day and make sure I think about what it says for a few minutes. It reads:

"You must be the change you wish to see in the world."

That one quote, that one small gift— perhaps she gave it to me as a sign of appreciation, maybe she saw it and knew I was changing and saw how relevant it was, whatever the reason— that she put that into my life has done amazing things, and this is where my journey really begins.

2

Gandhi Changed My Life

"You must be the change you wish to see in the world."

MAHATMA GANDHI

When my wife gave me that little Gandhi quote it had a dramatic impact on my life. When I looked at it for the first time, it struck me deeply right away.

That was the first time that I'd ever really understood anything about Mahatma Gandhi. I knew he was a religious leader, and I knew he'd been through a lot of strife in his life. I knew he'd been persecuted, but I never really understood his significance. That quote that gift from my wife Julie was the pivotal point in the complete shift to where I am today.

Before I got that little gift, I had started to see what my problems were. I had tremendous pain over the realization that I had so much changing to do if I was to become the person I so desperately desired to be. I had a mentor who gave me an idea of the bad side. Now I'd begun to see the good side with heart-driven leaders such as Juan Carlos and Gandhi. I can't begin to express the emotional impact this saying had on me.

Even before I knew anything about Gandhi, that quote blew my mind. It really hit me. I'd lived through being really poor and I was determined to do better for my kids. I knew that I had been a terrible person and I wanted to change that too. Gandhi summed it all up in one sentence.

I think Gandhi meant much more when he said, "You must be the change you wish to see in the world."

My interpretation is that you have to be accountable for any and all change you want to see in your life and in your world.

Everybody has issues. We all have trials we have to go through. But the many people that I've studied and learned about have demonstrated that you *can* make those changes. You *can* break those trends in your family, in your generation. If there is something about you that you don't like and you want to make things different, you *can* change it.

This quote has become synonymous with Gandhi and is known around the world. I think it means that anything you wish for, you can have, as long as you're willing to be accountable for making it happen. That's the way I took it, and that point of view has become me a real inspiration to me.

The little gift from my wife that I look at and think about every day led to a burning desire in me to study as many incredible leaders' lives as I could. Reading and rereading that quote gives me guidance and inspired me to put together a 10-point list of traits that I began to focus on and will focus on every day for the rest of my life.

Now it's time for you to meet a few of my mentors.

Mahatma Gandhi

Because of the quote, I started to do research about Gandhi. I wanted to find out everything I could about him.

I was immediately amazed at who and how Mahatma Gandhi was as a person. Yes, he was a religious leader. He was persecuted often and by many, yet all he was trying to do was praise and worship his God. And in spite of the persecution, millions and millions of people followed him and hundreds of millions more have been inspired by him. He didn't own anything, but he was rich beyond our wildest imagination.

What stands out most for me was his perseverance— the man's tenacity was incredible.

Mahatma Gandhi has become one of the most pivotal figures in all of Indian history. From the day he was born, he was always pushing for the things he absolutely believed in. He condemned corrupt governments. He condemned dictators. He encouraged his people to boycott the sale of British goods. He stepped out on a limb for the people that he loved, and he was persecuted in the process. Imprisoned. Cast aside. Punished.

Yet, in spite of everything he never spoke ill of others. He stayed true to his beliefs— his spiritual beliefs, his beliefs in independence, and his beliefs in the rights and dignity of mankind.

Because he believed so strongly in his religion, he pushed for freedom in the practice of that religion. Gandhi was so instrumental in assisting India to become what it is today that it cost him his life. There was an initial assassination attempt on Gandhi's life on January 20, 1948, and just 10 days later, he was killed by a fanatic. More than sixty years after his death, he is still loved and revered by millions of people, and his impact and influence survives him.

41

When I studied Gandhi, I found out that he attributed some of who he was to great guidance from his mentors.

He didn't care about wealth. He didn't care about riches. (He did care about prosperity, though, which is significant.) He cared deeply about other people. He had an unstoppable ability to get out there and create change. There was nobody else willing to do what he did, and he took action for no other reason than a strong inherent desire and belief in what was right and just. Gandhi served other people in an incredible way.

My study of Gandhi led me to Mother Teresa, and from there I studied other leaders in religion, politics, and business. That's how I developed a short list of 10 things that I wanted to focus on for the rest of my life. (You'll find this list at the end of this chapter.) For me, this is where things really started to take off in my life and work. Things began happening that were way beyond my own personal control.

Mother Teresa

I don't know how many of you have had a chance to really learn about Mother Teresa, but what I came to know about her is absolutely amazing to me.

She won the Nobel Peace Prize in 1979. She won more awards than any other religious leader, although she never asked for or sought any of them.

Like Gandhi, she was persecuted her entire life, and although many people loved her, there were others who absolutely did not like her at all.

I would argue that she might be one of the most influential business, political, and religious leaders of the world.

She spent most of her life striving to assist the poor, and most people remember her for the amazing work she accomplished with them. Many world governments actually tried to persecute and punish her for what she was doing, in spite of her completely unselfish service to others. Mother Teresa didn't have a cent to her name during her life, but she was definitely one of the richest leaders in the world.

Here's a quick story about how "rich" Mother Teresa really was.

She was sitting in hotel room in Los Angeles, California, when the phone rang and her assistant picked it up. It was a plea from a group in Seattle urgently requesting her presence that same night. Her assistant explained the request to Mother (she was called Mother by all who knew her) who said "Yes," immediately. "I'll be there."

Mother's assistant rolled her eyes, yet stifled her protest. Part of her job was to manage Mother's commitments and take care of her health and well-being. She called the airlines — all the airlines. Nothing was available. There was not one flight she could get on that would have them in Seattle that evening.

Mother simply smiled, saying "God will provide." Her assistant just shook her head.

A moment later, the phone rang again. It was an old friend of Mother's — a billionaire businessman who had supported her work for years. He had just called to say that he was in LA for a few days of meetings and his plane and crew were just sitting there and that if Mother needed anything, or wanted to go anywhere, it was hers for the asking.

Mother Teresa didn't have a cent to her name and she traveled the world five stars and always flew first class.

How'd she do that?

Mother Teresa had a core task that she focused on every day of her life –Worshiping her Lord and assisting the less fortunate. Everything else fell into place around that simple yet powerful commitment.

From the age of 12, Mother Teresa felt a strong calling from God. She knew from that young age that her place in the world was as a missionary, making the love of Christ known around the world. This was her core task.

At the age of 18, she left home and became a nun in an Irish community of sisters who did a lot of work in India. This was her calling.

And what were her reasons for what she did— what was her "Why"?

Her "Why" was simply and profoundly her love for God and her desire to assist the less fortunate. For the rest of her long life (she died at age 87) she never deviated from that once.

She just did it. She took action.

If she was ever seen in public anywhere, thousands of people rushed to her. It was amazing.

Mother Teresa had an incredible gravitational pull.

How about communication? This simple, unassuming nun was incredibly articulate and enabled all kinds of people to understand her message. She built trust like nobody else. She always gave credit to God and to other human mentors that assisted her. She always openly gave credit to others. Her whole life was dedicated to serving others. And she lived for each day, wholly present moment by moment.

Bill Gates

Bill Gates is another incredible leader that I studied. He started Microsoft with a dream years ago to create a computer that wasn't the size of a room, a personal computer that could sit on a desk. He enlisted the assistance of others, so that he could focus on that computer.

And he accomplished that by asking one question— a visionary question that would lead him to create one of the most remarkable, life and work changing achievements that would change the way the world does almost everything:

"What will it take to have a PC in every home in the world?"

And he kept that question in front of him, in his face, always.

Gates is arguably one of the most amazing computer gurus in the world. That's what he excels at. That's his pleasure, passion and purpose. So he could stay focused on what he does best, he brought in a business partner to be the driving force of the actual business-of-the-business of Microsoft.

Bill Gates has always been an incredible philanthropist, not just now that he's one of the richest men in the world, but throughout his whole life. He's given back to every community he's lived in. He's always been of service to others. He's detail-oriented... living fully today in the moment... has this incredible pull with people...

And by studying him, those same qualities began to emerge and fall into place for me.

I looked at business leaders, and then I starting looking at some of my own friends— Juan Carlos Barrios, who taught me how to love people, and Michael Clouse, who taught me about recruiting and Network Marketing. I started to study their qualities, their traits, and I saw the same fit everywhere I looked. It was almost surreal.

I went back to religion and politics, though, because I wanted to find out if there was a very specific leadership style and a roadmap that would fit any paradigm I would encounter. I wanted to take any great leader in the world and see if I could fit them into my 10 categories.

So, I had to drill down into...

Warren Buffett

I've always had an enormous admiration for Warren Buffett.

Warren Buffett is the CEO of Berkshire Hathaway, a conglomerate holding company. He also owns three Network Marketing/Direct Selling companies. And here's what he's directly quoted as saying about that;

"The best investment I've ever made."

He's an absolutely amazing man. He came from very humble beginnings, but along the way he discovered a passion for investing, and he always stayed true to that. He's never deviated from this. He's become one of the most successful investors in the world. That's Warren Buffet's core task.

With Berkshire Hathaway, Buffett stays focused on actual investing. He hires CEOs and managers and surrounds them with people to fill in their gaps. It's an incredible strategy. Warren Buffett, like the other leaders I've studied, has a reason for what he does that's insurmountable and unassailable. It's unstoppable, bigger than anything you could ever imagine.

Warren Buffett has an amazing ability to captivate people when he's around them and when he speaks. He's a man of few words, but when he speaks, people listen. He has an ability to get a point across that's second to none.

This ability is due to the incredible trust and mentorship he's built into his life.

It's worth noting that somebody as significant and successful as Warren Buffet openly gives credit to his mentors. He's also a very generous philanthropist. He doesn't have to share his investment information and prowess with competitors and governments around the world— but he does. And in his business, his service to others is beyond impressive.

Steve Jobs

Steve Jobs is another incredible leader. He started Apple computers, which turned into a company that's revolutionized the music industry (iPod) mobile phone business (iPhone) and turned laptops into tablets (iPad). Not to mention Mac and Pixar with *Finding Nemo, Toy Story* and more. What a great story he has! In spite of his own personal adversities, he just keeps going forward.

I found out that Steve, like all leaders at some point in their lives, came under incredible criticism and skepticism. He was even fired from the company he started!

Now, whether that's good or bad is not the point. What's important is his incredible ability to stay focused and get the jobs (pun intended) done in spite of some incredible frustrations and rejections in his own life.

One of the things that gave me solace as I studied Steve Jobs and all these leaders was the fact that at some point in their lives every one of them was completely abandoned by most of the people around them— with the exception of a trusted few that stuck with them through everything.

This reminded me of my own journey. After that first year in Network Marketing most of the people in my life abandoned me. And, like Steve Jobs, a few incredible ones stuck with me.

I'm not placing myself "up there" with these great leaders. I'm working on those 40 things I've identified and I'll be doing that for a long time. But it is very reassuring to realize that they'd been through similar types of tribulations.

I guarantee that some of you reading this book right now are feeling the same way. You might be at a point in your life where you've been trying really hard, but you've been abandoned by most everybody around you. I hope that my sharing this makes you realize that tomorrow is a new day, and there will be other people in your life. Some of the greatest leaders in the world have had to rebuild everything.

Here's a piece of Steve Jobs' story that inspired me to keep going— and taught me a life lesson about love and loss. (It's from the Commencement he gave at Stanford University on June 12, 2005.)

"I was lucky— I found what I loved to do early in life. Woz and I started Apple in my parent's garage when I was 20. We worked hard, and in 10 years Apple had grown from just the two of us in a garage into a $2 billion company with over 4000 employees. We had just released our finest creation— the Macintosh— a year earlier, and I had just turned 30. And then I got fired. How can you get fired from a company you started?

Well, as Apple grew we hired someone who I thought was very talented to run the company with me, and for the first year or so things went well. But then our visions of the future began to diverge and eventually we had a falling out. When we did, our Board of Directors sided with him.

So at 30 I was out. And very publicly out. What had been the focus of my entire adult life was gone, and it was devastating.

I really didn't know what to do for a few months. I felt that I had let the previous generation of entrepreneurs down— that I had dropped the baton as it was being passed to me. I met with David Packard and Bob Noyce and tried to apologize for screwing up so badly. I was a very public failure, and I even thought about running away from the valley. But something slowly began to dawn on me— I still loved what I did. The turn of events at Apple had not changed that one bit. I had been rejected, but I was still in love. And so I decided to start over.

I didn't see it then, but it turned out that getting fired from Apple was the best thing that could have ever happened to me. The heaviness of being successful was replaced by the lightness of being a beginner again, less sure about everything. It freed me to enter one of the most creative periods of my life.

During the next five years, I started a company named NeXT, another company named Pixar, and fell in love with an amazing woman who would become my wife. Pixar went on to create the world's first computer animated feature film, Toy Story, and is now the most successful animation studio in the world. In a remarkable turn of events, Apple bought NeXT, I returned to Apple, and the technology we developed at NeXT is at the heart of Apple's current renaissance. And Laurene and I have a wonderful family together.

I'm pretty sure none of this would have happened if I hadn't been fired from Apple. It was awful- tasting medicine, but I guess the patient needed it.

Sometimes life hits you in the head with a brick. Don't lose faith.

I'm convinced that the only thing that kept me going was that I loved what I did. You've got to find what you love. And that is as true for your work as it is for your lovers. Your work is going to fill a large part of your life, and the only way to be truly satisfied is to do what you believe is great work. And the only way to do great work is to love what you do.

If you haven't found it yet, keep looking. Don't settle. As with all matters of the heart, you'll know when you find it. And, like any great relationship, it just gets better and better as the years roll on. So keep looking until you find it. Don't settle."

Wow!

In our business we always tell people that they must be anchored to a reason for what they do… a reason so deep, so personal, that even on the worst days when they want to quit, this reason will keep them going. My childhood and my dad's death are my reasons. I found out that all leaders have their own deep reasons.

I became really intrigued as I saw compelling similarities in absolutely opposite-end-of-the-spectrum types of leaders. Religion, politics, business… the same core qualities were present in every one of the leaders in each of these fields. There are lots of other leadership qualities, and others have written books on them. But I've narrowed it down to 10 that really got my attention. I began asking myself, "Have I found a roadmap for myself?" I believed I had, and I wasn't finished yet.

I looked at other businesses, because I'm just enthralled with business. As you learned in the first chapter, I have a disease; it's called Chronic Entrepreneur Syndrome (CES). I want to be a great business leader. I want to be remembered as a great business leader, but the right type of leader: A visionary leader. A visionary leader like...

John F. Kennedy

One of my mentors shared with me his theory that there are really only two types of leaders in the world: Dictators and heart-driven leaders. That mentor used John F. Kennedy as an example of a leader that leads from the heart. I began to read all I could about John F. Kennedy.

As I developed my own leadership skill, I wanted to be perceived as somebody like JFK. He was loved and revered by millions of people. He had a very soft leadership style, which was evident in how he operated every day. He was probably one of the most caring presidents America has ever known. He was an incredibly heart-led person. He had a real ability to attract people and have people love him. I'm sure that's because he loved them.

Kennedy had some really significant events happen in his childhood that drove him through the rest of his life. He was incredibly articulate, a powerful speaker, and he had an amazing ability to build trust in those around him.

I found some powerful similarities between Gandhi and Kennedy

It's interesting that both Gandhi and John F. Kennedy were assassinated at very young ages. Both of them had similar leadership characteristics. Both of them had an incredible desire to follow a unique path, and both of them were completely focused on one thing in each of their lives— helping people.

They each discovered what I call their "core task."

Once they identified their driving force, their core task, they stuck to it. They never deviated from it, no matter what. Both of them had this amazing "gravitational pull," which is another phrase I came up with to describe that quality to attract others leaders have.

When these men walked into a room people noticed. They each had smiles that were engaging and captivating. People wanted to be around them. I believe people could feel their hearts. And both of them had this amazing ability to communicate— verbally and nonverbally.

Neither of them had ever taken specific training in communication, but they were really great at saying what was on their mind and speaking in general. They knew how to use intonation.

Each had this incredible ability to gain and give trust and loyalty.

Both Gandhi and Kennedy were supremely confident, and both of them attributed much of their success to having powerful mentors.

I was amazed at how similar these two men were.

Even though they were from different periods of time and different sides of the world, both of them committed their entire lives to serving others. They both were very detail-oriented and able to balance lots of things in their lives at the same time. They were excellent multi-taskers, and regardless of the pressures around them, they had the ability to stay present and live in the now.

I wanted to be somebody that could truly assist millions of people to achieve success. I began to realize that I was creating a formula for becoming the kind of leader I wanted to be.

Last but not at all least...

Pierre Trudeau

Pierre Trudeau was one of Canada's greatest prime ministers. He reminds me a lot of John F. Kennedy. He was flamboyant and extremely charismatic. That same gravitational pull existed in him.

He had an incredible core task. Pierre Trudeau was instrumental in bringing the Canadian Charter of Rights and Freedoms into being.

Canada was a British Colony that became independent under the British North America Act. After many years, there was an uprising and a division in Canada. As Prime Minister, Trudeau was able to bring all the people together and move legislation through the House of Commons that led to the greatest law of Canada's history, the Canadian Charter of Rights and Freedoms.

He was often highly criticized, but he led through love and created a high degree of trust.

Lessons Learned

After studying these seven world leaders, I was blown away by how much they all had in common. I couldn't believe that in spite of being from such different worlds, so many different walks of life, they possessed the same core values and so many of the same personality traits.

Starting from that simple gift from my wife, a true roadmap for success had been revealed to me. Since then, I have focused on these 10 Traits of Inspirational Leaders. By applying them to my life I've been able to create incredible wealth with deeper, stronger relationships and partnerships than I have ever had before.

Prosperity is a very significant word for me. Prosperity to religious leaders means something different than it means to business and political leaders. All the leaders I've mentioned stayed absolutely core-focused on their core task.

I found that all of these leaders stayed focused, determined their core task, and identified what brought them prosperity.

Now, in Network Marketing, the core task is prospecting and introducing new people to our business. But in other businesses the core task is different. For instance, Warren Buffett's core task is investing. Bill Gate's core task is computer programming. In John F. Kennedy's and Pierre Trudeau's worlds, the core task was politics. And in Mother Teresa's world, it was serving God.

Trust me, if you apply these 10 traits to your life, even the sky won't be your limit!

These leaders all stayed focused;

    1.   These leaders all stayed focused;

2. They were all motivated by incredible reasons for what they did;

3. They all had this ability to pull people towards them;

4. They were able to communicate powerfully and persuasively;

5. They had the ability to build and give trust;

6. They had confidence in their calling;

7. They were teachable, openly seeking out and finding mentors always ready to give credit to those mentors;

8. They were all detail-oriented and multi-taskers;

9. They all had the ability to live in the moment of now;

And ...

They remained humble and in service to others no matter what.

This is a *very* important point. I noticed that all of these inspirational leaders were consistently shot down and criticized by other people, yet the adversity was like water off a duck's back for them. They never let it get to them. And even to their biggest critics, they gave back love in return.

What happened next was really exciting for me.

Three Types of Leadership

I remembered the words from one of my mentors about there being two types of leaders (dictators and heartfelt leaders), and I thought about how I just never felt complete with that idea. I didn't believe that there were just two types of leaders. I've always believed *we are all born leaders.*

Think about this: When children are born, the mannerisms they develop, the way they talk, the way they act, all come from their parents. Parents are leaders. *Any ability for one human being to affect another human being is truly leadership.*

That's where I got the idea that there were actually *three* types of leaders. I believe that there are three types and WE ARE ALL leaders in one of three ways:

Authoritarian ♦ Complacent ♦ Inspirational

In order to make this simpler to understand, I've detailed these three types of leaders in a later chapter and given you some easy-to-follow ideas so you can see exactly which type you are. Once you've identified precisely where you fit it is as easy as applying the 10 Traits of Inspirational Leadership to your life and watching yourself progress.

The Value of Having a Roadmap

We all lead busy lives. We are each at different stages of our development. Some of you may be feeling the pain of abandonment and rejection right now. Maybe you are tired of always trying to put your best foot forward and stumbling. Since you've read this far, you know I understand.

That's why I began studying leaders and identifying the traits they had in common. I wanted more and better in every area of my life.

The goal is for all of us to achieve prosperity beyond our wildest dreams, with legions of friends and colleagues that trust us and love us.

You can benefit from incredible mentors in your lives and you can master Network Marketing in the process.

Regardless of where you're at right now, what you have going on in your life, or how big your own business is, once you start applying the 10 traits covered in this chapter, you'll be on your way to obtaining whatever level of prosperity you desire. You do that simply by switching your focus from acquiring money to developing the 10 traits of inspirational leadership in your life. I know you can do that, because that's what I did, and... it works!

In the coming chapters, you'll learn where you fit onto the leadership continuum, exactly what the 10 traits of inspirational leadership are and how to apply them to your life. You'll also learn what the secrets to success are and what pitfalls to avoid along the way.

Let's begin.

Inspired Actions

Seven Inspirational Leaders

1. Mahatma Gandhi

2 Mother Teresa

3. Bill Gates

4. Warren Buffett

5. Steve Jobs

6. John F. Kennedy

7. Pierre Trudeau

The 10 Traits of Inspirational Leaders

1. Have a mentor – Be a mentor

2. Be the best at your core task

3. Have a "Why" that makes you cry

4. Be an excellent communicator

5. Be supremely confident

6. Be detail-oriented and learn to multitask

7. Have a strong gravitational pull

8. Serve others: Inspire trust and loyalty

9. Live in the present moment

10. Be action driven/Led

3

Three Types of Leadership

"You must be the change you wish to see in the world."

SIR ISSAC NEWTON

We are all born with leadership potential. In most people, that potential remains under-developed or undeveloped. The questions to ask yourself are:

**Do you want to be small,
or do you want to be great?**

**Do you want to be okay,
or do you want to be amazing?**

**Do you want to be average,
or do you want to be exceptional?**

I see leadership as a continuum. At one end of the continuum is the biggest group of leaders. At the other end of the continuum are the leaders I've profiled. I call those folks "Inspirational Leaders," because they absolutely inspire me.

We Are All Born Leaders

Now, you might say, "I'm a follower not a leader." If so, here's something for you to think about.

Have you ever known a father who was in the military and his son joined the military, too (like me)? Or how about a parent who isn't the most energetic person in the world, a parent who ends up on the couch every day after dinner? More often than not, if you take a look at complacency in a parent you'll see complacency in their children.

There are parents that are lethargic and don't want to go anywhere. There are parents that don't have good eating habits. There's a way better than average chance that their children will end up the same way. That's an example of leadership too.

If your example influences another person to do the same thing, you're a leader.

My wife is a great example of leadership. She is a true inspiration in my life. Julie's down to earth. Very humble. She's not materialistic, things just don't matter to her. Julie is so grounded it's incredible. And our children, thank God, are becoming just like that.

The Leadership Continuum – 3 Types of Leaders

As I began to study leadership I discovered that there are three basic types of leaders and three basic leadership styles.

In 1939, psychologist Kurt Lewin led a group of researchers in a study designed to identify the different styles of leadership. Over the years further research has uncovered more specific types of leadership, but this early study laid the groundwork establishing these three major leadership styles: *laissez-faire, authoritarian,* and *democratic.*

As I continued my study, I refined the categories for myself this way: *complacent, authoritarian,* and *inspirational.* We are all one of those three.

Complacent Leadership

This is the biggest category of leaders and is made up of 90% of the people in the world. These are leaders who just meander aimlessly through life. They are the nine-to-fivers who don't do any more than they have to— Ever.

These are individuals that just sort of drift along. You might not think they should be called leaders at all, but as I mentioned earlier, if others follow them and emulate their behavior, then they are leaders. They don't know it. Neither does anyone else.

Authoritarian Leaders

Next there are the authoritarian leaders. These are leaders who are very strong and aggressive. Their hidden motto is "Do as I say, not as I do."

An example of an authoritarian leader who has done incredibly well in life is Lee Iacocca of the Chrysler Corporation and author *of Where Have All the Leaders Gone?*

Mr. Iacocca ruled with an iron fist. It was his way or the highway. He had a *very* authoritarian style. He's been quoted as saying that there is one word to describe a successful manager: Decisiveness. And that's the way he operated.

Did he get results? Yes, he did.

Would people follow him to Hell and back?

You know the answer to that. Where is he now? *Gone.* Like all of his type of leader.

He believed that you had to be able to think on your feet. He took risks and wasn't afraid of making unpopular decisions, with little or no feedback from his superiors, peers, or subordinates.

Really terrible authoritarian leaders are called dictators.

Remember what my two key leaders called me on Christmas Eve?

Hitler was one of those. Genghis Khan is another example. They are unreasonable in their demands, believe that all the decision-making power is theirs alone, and they do not allow others to question decisions or their authority. These are the worst of the worst.

Authoritarian leadership is often appropriate in emergencies and extreme situations— I learned this in law enforcement— but it tends to be disempowering and frustrating to those who must answer to this type of leader day after day. Okay for a cop sometimes. Not a spouse, parent or Network Marketer.

Inspirational Leaders

At the opposite end of the continuum are those leaders that are loved by everybody. They're not perfect. But these leaders embody the 10 traits, and their leadership comes from the heart

As Green Bay Packers' coach Vince Lombardi once said, "Leadership is based on a spiritual quality; the power to inspire, the power to inspire others to follow."

John F. Kennedy exhibited this type of leadership. He had a keen understanding of people that led him to express a genuine warmth and affection, yet he was aware and calculating at the same time. He respected those who worked for him and with him, but he was also quick to assess where each individual would fit best and be the most effective and best utilized.

Kennedy was a great communicator— and he made it easy for others to communicate with him. His speeches are some of the most inspiring of any politician, past or present. John F. Kennedy had a special ability to energize those he led. Like all pure energy that "gravitational pull" I told you about, has an equal and opposite reaction as well. Gravitational *push.*

The 10 Traits of Inspirational Leaders

As I studied the seven world leaders mentioned in Chapter Two, I saw that they each possessed these ten traits. It was amazing to me, because they came from uniquely different walks of life.

When I started to look at the leaders in my own life that I admired, I saw the traits almost like musical notes jumping off the sheet.

> **I knew that if I started to apply these 10 traits, I couldn't help but be a better person, and I would start to achieve the success I was looking for in life.**

My heartfelt belief is that if YOU apply these ten traits to your life, you too can achieve whatever level of prosperity you desire.

1. Have a mentor – Be a mentor

Don't reinvent the wheel. Seek out coaches and mentors who are where you want to be and be open and willing to listen to them and do what they say.

Make sure you choose trustworthy mentors. That's hard to do sometimes, but, it's required. When you achieve success, others will seek you out for mentorship and you'll be able to provide them with a proven path to achieving their goals and dreams.

2. Be the best at your core task

All the leaders I studied had a single focus that carried them from the early days of their enterprises into their successful futures. In Network Marketing, **your core task is prospecting**. This is your main focus, and like all top leaders you don't want to deviate from it.

Develop your skills, become the greatest prospector in the world, and watch your business soar!

3. Have a "Why" that makes you cry

Even after all these years, my "Why" can still move me to tears. It doesn't matter that I've reached many of my goals— thinking about my own experiences as a child continues to motivate me to create a very different life for my children, no matter what! Your "Why" should have this same power and intensity. If it doesn't, then dig deeper to come up with one that does.

4. Be an excellent communicator

Leaders communicate. Becoming a skilled communicator is essential. Ours is a business of connecting with people, and no matter what your personality type, you can learn to create rapport and interact with others. Words are powerful— learn to use them effectively.

5. Be supremely confident

All the leaders I studied had a high degree of self-confidence. They each encountered many obstacles and lots of rejection along the way, but they didn't let this affect their morale. Each in their own way was bold, courageous, unflappable and full of determination and tenacity. Your path to the top will require this as well.

You build confidence by building belief.

In my book, *The Most Important Minute,* you will find an entire chapter about building confidence by building belief. It's that important.

6. Be detail-oriented and learn to multitask

One trait of all great leaders is the ability to be organized, pay attention to details, and multitask. Life is full of interruptions and the urgent will always be louder than the truly important. On your path to leadership make sure you have a system in place that supports your focus and drives you forward.

7. Have a strong gravitational pull

Leaders in every field have an incredible ability to pull people towards them. People are just naturally drawn to them. This comes from being congruent and living from the inside out, as well as having a deep sense of compassion for others. The more you connect with your own unique calling and abilities, the more others will just naturally be drawn to you too.

8. Serve others: Inspire trust and loyalty

Leaders inspire others to trust them. They have many loyal followers not because they use force or exert control over others, but because they have chosen to serve others. This type of leader has learned to leave his or her ego at the door and put other people first.

9. Live in the present moment

All leaders are visionaries, but they aren't so focused on the future that they aren't fully engaged in the present moment. On the contrary, they experience the present in all its fullness. When you are with one of these leaders, you clearly sense they are living in the now, even while they are working to achieve future goals. On your own journey make sure you experience each and every day to the max.

10. Be action driven

Achieving your goals involves knowing what you want and then taking the necessary action to make success happen. Be a "Do It Now" kind of person. Learn from the powerful examples of the Inspirational Leaders I studied, and create the success you dream of.

Your Own Leadership Style

Regardless of where you are on the continuum, you can begin to focus on your own journey toward inspirational leadership. Understanding the three types of leaders and the 10 traits of inspirational leaders you want to model will provide the roadmap to success that you can easily follow.

4

Find a Great Mentor

"I was lucky to have the right heroes. Tell me who your heroes are and I'll tell you how you'll turn out to be. The qualities of the one you admire are the traits that you, with a little practice, can make your own, and that, if practiced, will become habit-forming."

WARREN BUFFETT

If you are really serious about being successful, *find a great mentor*.

A good mentor is not necessarily the biggest income earner in your company, either. Find somebody who is successful, but make sure that individual has the same ethical principles and morals you admire and aspire. Don't be afraid to interview a few people before you choose somebody to follow, and until you're making a huge paycheck, don't be afraid to be a follower. *Be coachable.*

When you have big goals, it's much easier to follow in the footsteps of others than to create your own path.

Picture a northern Canadian morning. You look out your window and see three feet of fresh snow outside. Imagine trying to walk through that snow all by yourself— you're up to your waist in it, struggling along. As you pull your feet out of the deep snow, one slow, strenuous step at a time, your boot nearly comes off. *It's hard!*

Now, think about how much easier it would be if somebody else has already walked where you wanted to go. All you have to do is walk in their footprints each step of the way. How much easier would that be?

This is exactly what our business is about. If you want to build it big, follow somebody else's footsteps. Never stop learning and always stay coachable.

Warren Buffett's Mentor

Warren Buffett, the world's greatest investor and one of the Inspirational Leaders I studied, credits much of his success to his mentors. When he began his investing career, he was mentored by an Englishman named Benjamin Graham, who is often referred to as the dean of financial analysis.

Graham was born in London in 1894 and moved to New York City with his parents when he was one year old. He graduated from Columbia University as salutatorian of his class with a BS degree at age 20 and started his financial career on Wall Street as a messenger. He worked his way up through the company, eventually becoming a full partner.

Graham was earning $600,000 a year by the time he was 25 years old— and this was in 1919! That's literally millions in today's dollars. Although his firm survived the stock market crash in 1929, Graham lost his personal fortune. He was determined to recreate his financial success and teach others to do the same. His goal became teaching investors how to build wealth in a conservative and rational manner. He taught that investing is a discipline— one that takes research, training, and experience.

Warren Buffett began absorbing Ben Graham's simple yet profound investment principles at the age of 21, and he was captivated by this financial expert.

Buffett discovered that his mentor was the chairman of a then small, unknown insurance company named GEICO. One Saturday morning he took a train to Washington, D.C. to find the company's headquarters. When he got there, the doors were locked. Unstoppable, Buffett began pounding on the door until a janitor opened it for him. He asked if there was anyone in the building. There was. Loren Davidson, the vice president of finance, was working on the sixth floor.

Buffett went to find him and when he did, he began questioning him about the company and its business practices. The conversation lasted four hours. That meeting with Davidson led to Buffett being mentored by Ben Graham, an experience that stayed with Buffett for the rest of his life. He even named his son, Howard Graham Buffett in honor of his mentor. Eventually Buffett acquired GEICO through his corporation, Berkshire Hathaway. He never fails to acknowledge what he learned from Graham and describes Graham's book, *The Intelligent Investor* as "the best book about investing ever written."

Early Mentors

I've always known the value of having a mentor. When I was on the SWAT team, we always had a team leader. He was the most senior guy on the team.

Now, being on a SWAT team is dangerous at all times. One bad decision could cost someone's life— my own or one of my partner's. We worked as a unified team and we *always* followed the directions of the team leader— we *always* trusted his advice. And we followed that advice explicitly, because doing so could mean the difference between life and death.

For example, I learned from my SWAT team leader how best to enter a building. Following his lead, when we went in I would veer off to the left, clear a room, and wait there. Even though my instincts might have told me not to wait, by opening the next door too soon I could throw off the entire plan and somebody could get hurt.

I learned to follow the advice of the leader, even if my own instincts told me something different.

I managed to stay alive and unhurt throughout my SWAT team experience, and so did everyone else on our team. We achieved every outcome we planned— whether it was freeing hostages or boarding ships or successfully raiding drug houses. Knowing that people with guns and knives were on the other sides of those doors, following the advice and direction of my team leader and acting on his experience was crucial. It was this ability to act on somebody else's experience with complete trust that kept me alive. The lessons I learned on the SWAT team have guided me through the rest of my life.

My first real experience having a business mentor was when I opened my mortgage company back in 2001. I didn't know much about the mortgage industry, but I knew of some very successful mortgage brokers in Ottawa where I was living. Being the brazen guy I can be, I called up the top mortgage broker in town, because I was determined to build a huge mortgage business and make a fortune. I wanted to make more money than this top broker did. I told her straight out, "I want to learn everything I can about mortgages. I've always gone right to the top in anything I've done."

Her response? She laughed hysterically at me over the phone. I'll never forget that. Of course, I asked what anyone would ask when somebody laughs at you for asking an honest question: "Why are you laughing?"

Her answer was very simple:

"Kid, why the heck would I ever train my competition?"

She continued, "You've got to be out to lunch! You really ought to just quit while you're ahead. You're just going to hurt yourself."

I said, "Why do you say that?"

She said, "Because you're coming to *me* looking for advice. Fish shouldn't swim with sharks."

I laughed right back at her, and I retorted with another question. "Hey, listen, what if I pay you?"

She said, "What are you talking about?"

I said, "I'll give you $10,000 for just one day if you'll promise to tell me honestly every single thing I need to do to be successful in the mortgage industry."

She laughed again, but she agreed. I don't know to this day why she agreed, because that wasn't a lot of money for her, but we spent one very incredible day together. She literally opened up to me, telling me everything she knew about mortgages. In turn, I applied every bit of that advice.

She encouraged me to focus on relationships.

She told me that if I wanted create a significant business in the mortgage industry, then I should build relationships with real

71

estate agents and other referral sources and not worry about individual mortgages. She taught me that if I treated those people honestly and ethically and built friendships and partnerships with them, they would provide me with the mortgages I was seeking to arrange.

She also told me to be very accurate with my paperwork. Now, I hated paperwork, but because of that advice I learned to keep accurate notes and records. I learned to pick just a couple of key lenders to work with and refer all my business. She advised me to get to know the loan officers and become familiar with the conditions those banks offered. Following her advice, I became an expert in these areas.

I did everything she told me, and I started to make just as much money as she did. Two years later, because of this mentor, I was earning over a million dollars a year. And I was able to build my mortgage business part-time while I was still a homicide detective. I had nine full-time employees, and we funded hundreds of millions of dollars in mortgages.

What was ironic about this whole experience is that I did become my mentor's competitor, but she never looked at it that way. We became great friends, and she began coaching me on real estate investments and other areas related to the mortgage industry. I still have a relationship with her to this day although I don't deal with her as much now. It's important for you to know that the mentors you have at one stage in your life probably will not be your mentors for your entire life. You'll go in different directions, you'll follow different roads, and you'll acquire new mentors along the way.

A short time ago I met a man named Derek Baird. Derek owns several real estate practices. He's built offices from the ground up. He's a real estate investor, and he's made millions and millions of dollars for himself. He's written books on mentorship, and currently he mentors many people.

As I developed a friendship with him, we talked about the subject of mentorship and how important it was. He gives credit to his mentors for all of his success, which is amazing because he has been such an inspiration to me.

One of the things he taught me is that when you choose a mentor, the relationship should serve both of you.

What he means is that when you're looking for a mentor, obviously you're seeking advice to assist you to be more successful or prosperous, but your mentor also requires something out of that relationship.

This has served me in many ways. In my experience, I've had mentors that I thought had pure intentions. I thought they just wanted to assist me, but I found out afterwards they were using me for their own purpose and I discovered that they lied to me in the process. They definitely had something in it for themselves, although they told me they didn't. I've had other mentors who told me right up front what was in it for them.

If you're looking for a mentor, make sure that it's a win/win situation for both of you. Otherwise, neither of you will receive the full potential from that mentorship.

Be Careful Who You Choose as Your Mentor

My experience with mentorship in Network Marketing began during my first couple of months in the business. As I started to do well, a millionaire in my upline offered to coach me. I was blinded by his success, so I began following his lead without ever questioning him. He told me that if I wanted to make a million dollars in Network Marketing, I had to do *exactly* what he told me and *never* doubt him.

I was so enthralled by Network Marketing and with the potential to make millions in residual income that I followed him without question.

Little did I know, but he was a tyrant. He was one of the worst dictators I've ever encountered, but I never saw it until it was too late.

He advised me to forget about people, that success was all about business volume. He coached me to build my business knowing that there would always be people that would let me down.

People in my organization would come to me with challenges and frustrations, and he would tell me to just forget about them.

I remember him saying, "Forget about that person. They're just going to drag you down. There's no potential in that person." I wanted so badly to be successful that I just followed his lead.

He also used to dangle gifts in front of me all the time. He'd buy me lunch, or he'd buy me a new suit or tie. He was always reminding me of all the things he did for me and all the reasons I should be loyal to him. He made an example of me to others in such an arrogant way that people started to hate me. I hung out with him so much and modeled his behavior that I developed the same personality traits he had.

As I mentioned in the first chapter, by the end of my first year in Network Marketing some very important people in my life abandoned me because I was becoming too much like that mentor. They told me I was becoming a dictator.

Finally, I saw it. It was a very painful experience. But now at least I had an example of what I didn't want to be like as a leader and as a mentor, and I immediately broke away from that man.

The Right Kind of Mentor

Not long after this experience, another mentor came in my life and assisted me with releasing the negative emotions I had created. This individual really started opening my eyes to Inspirational Leadership.

He taught me that there are two types of leaders.

"There are dictators," he said, "and you know who they are. Your old mentor was one. The worst dictator I know of was Adolf Hitler. He murdered millions of people who didn't conform to his ways. He's the most extreme example of a dictator leader."

While Hitler and others like him (i.e., Genghis Khan, Joseph Stalin, Idi Amin) are the extreme, there are other authoritarian leaders who lead with an iron fist. Their philosophy is "Do as I say and not as I do." Their chosen method of motivation is belittling and berating people into submission.

My new mentor went on to say, "There are also incredible leaders like John F. Kennedy who rule through love. Kennedy led with respect, and he won the hearts of millions of people in the process. Ken you have a choice. You can either be a dictator, or you can rule through love, respect and trust."

This mentor shared much wisdom and advice with me over the next couple of years, and he led me in a direction that really assisted me to become who I am and to earn the income that I earn today. But guess what?

autonomyBEING THE CHANGE – INSPIRED to WIN in NETWORK MARKETING

Once again I became blinded to the truth about my mentor.

I never knew what he was really after, even though one of the things I found very peculiar was that when we first started to work together he demanded to be my only mentor. He also said if ever I was in any other business, he required I give him the option to be above me in that business. In return for his years of wisdom, I had to agree to this and never challenge it.

Because he gave me such great advice about leadership, I agreed. It worked well for a while, but eventually I discovered the reality of who he was. I found out that he had lied about some important things from his past.

He became very aggressive with me, demanding that I stick with my commitment to him. But I realized in my heart that he had his own motives and they were incongruent with mine. I became aware that he was using me. Behind the scenes he was doing unethical things to try and make as much money as he could. When it became evident that he didn't really care about people, I broke away from him.

This was another very painful experience, because I owe part of my success today to this mentor. In spite of that, I couldn't be loyal to him because his heart wasn't in the right place. I saw that he was just out for himself, and fortunately I chose to walk away from him in time.

While I learned a lot from these two mentors and I respect them for that, at the same time they were both tyrants with ulterior motives and I just couldn't continue to be mentored by either of them.

Coming out of my experience with that second mentor, Derek Baird gave me just the right advice at the time when he told me, "There's got to be something in it for both the mentor and

76

the student. If somebody's telling you there isn't, don't mentor with that person. Be very suspicious of them."

No mentor knows everything. If you're choosing a mentor, make sure that there's something in it for both of you.

Always find mentors that have the success you're looking for in the field you're in.

When you're with a mentor, always be very respectful of that mentor's time. If you ask your mentor for advice and then don't take it, then shame on you. If you're wasting their time, that mentor has every right to not to want to mentor you anymore. I've never met a mentor who is not an extremely busy person.

Ideally, you should have several mentors in your life, depending on the areas you're seeking to master. I personally seek counsel from several mentors who are not involved in Network Marketing, and I still get advice from my original mentor, the mortgage broker, on real estate transactions.

Ask yourself, "Is the advice I'm getting from my mentor congruent with my own beliefs?" If the answer is no, then don't follow it. Stay true to yourself. It's important to continually ask yourself what your core beliefs and values are. Be clear about what you believe in the most and have that guide you.

Another important thing is to openly give credit to your mentors. Don't ever take the credit. Don't ever feel that *you* have to be the source of the advice you share. As you progress, your advice will be a lot more valid and valuable to others if they hear the story of how you got that advice in the first place. So, freely share that. If you're mentoring somebody, make sure that you give credit where credit is due.

When you find great mentors and begin to take advice from them, you'll become successful, and other people will start coming to you for advice.

Be very careful to not get into this mode too quickly. Don't offer advice to people unless you've truly succeeded at the level where you feel confident your advice can be taken the right way. There are way too many teachers out there today who have never experienced what they teach.

I see so many people giving advice to others particularly in Network Marketing. The saying, "Unless you've walked a mile in somebody's shoes..." should ring truly in your ears right now.

Make sure that the mentor you're looking for has actually walked down the road you're seeking to travel. This is very, *very* important.

As you start to become successful, you'll become known in your business, but don't become a mentor to others until you're truly achieving the success that you want. I can't tell you the amount of experiences I've been through where I've observed people giving advice to others when they haven't been successful themselves yet.

When you become a mentor, don't be afraid to coach somebody else, but take care and don't sacrifice yourself in the process. Remain a student at all times. Continue to search for more and better awareness and understanding, and you'll continually expand your own mastery and mentorship. Today I coach many, many people about Network Marketing, but I am first and always a student.

Through my own experience, I've learned it's important to tell a lot of stories. Don't simply give "how to" advice based on what you think is accurate. Look back through your own experiences, and if you have an example related to the advice you're giving, share that, and let your students come up with ideas or decisions based on the stories you tell.

Looking back at all the mentors I've had, the greatest advice was the stories they told about their own experiences. They always gave the credit to their mentors. I try to do the same thing every day, and you'll want to do this too.

Another quality of a great mentor is that they always remain receptive to receiving coaching personally. You'll never hear a great mentor say, "I know that already."

Orrin Woodward is one of the most successful Network Marketing leaders in the world. He has his own leadership development company and he co-wrote the NY Times, Wall Street Journal, Business Weekly, USA Today, and Money Magazine best seller, *Launching a Leadership Revolution.*

Orrin speaks on leadership and personal growth across the globe. His highly popular blog has received international acclaim as an Alltop Leadership Selection, HR's Top 100 Blogs for Management and Leadership, and a Universities Online Top 100 Leadership Blog.

Simply put, Orrin is an expert on the subject of leadership— and he literally puts his money where his mouth is by earning a very significant multi-million annual income practicing what he preaches leading and mentoring an international Networking organization of hundreds-of-thousands around the world.

Yet with all of that "financial and social proof" of his success and expertise, Orrin thinks of himself first as a student. He's always learning. Always reading new books. Always studying.

In fact, Orrin and his kids have a game they play where they're all reading the same book at the same time and they meet each afternoon to discuss the most important thing they've learned from the book that day. A prize is awarded for the most interesting and thoughtful report. And sometimes, but not all the time, Orrin wins.

Orrin Woodward's commitment to life-long learning inspires me.

I've come to greatly appreciate the wisdom of the following declaration and I apply it to every mentoring relationship I'm involved in:

"I will never lie to you and I will never knowingly have you do anything that is not in your best interests.'

It's a two-way street for both mentor and the person being mentored.

Inspired Actions

Tips to Finding the Right Mentors

- Be open to having several mentors.

- Understand what's in the relationship for both you and your mentor; make sure it's a win/win situation.

- Ask yourself if their beliefs and philosophy are congruent with your own ideals.

- Pick a mentor that can coach through personal stories and experiences.

- Choose a mentor that has mentors of his or her own.

- Make sure the mentor has walked down the path you are seeking to travel.

- Look for a mentor who is completely honest and ethical.

How to Steer Clear of the Wrong Mentors

- Be careful of mentors who make undue demands on you (unquestioning loyalty, for example).

- Don't get involved with mentors who are overly aggressive and controlling in their interactions with you.

- Be wary of any mentor whom you suspect of unethical business practices of any kind.

- Stay away from mentors who don't truly care about others.

- Never choose a mentor who you feel is dishonest about his past.

- Don't listen to a mentor who insists that you never question them.

_____

5

Prospecting Your Core Task

*"Smart, committed people with the right support
and vision can have a huge impact."*

BILL GATES

Leaders in every area of life have one significant common thread:

**They identified their core task early on,
and they stayed laser-focused on it.**

For the religious leaders I studied, their core task was love for God and service to others, period. They were presented with many other opportunities during the course of their lives, and they could have gone in other directions, but they made the choice and never deviated from this core calling.

The greatest business leaders in the world have also identified what they're the best at and stayed completely focused on that, even though they may be involved in other different businesses or projects.

For example, Bill Gates has authored a number of books and invested in other companies, but the core task as he identified it in early adulthood was designing computers. He never deviated from that until 2006 when he transitioned from full-time work at Microsoft to part-time, and began working full-time at the Bill & Melinda Gates Foundation. His core task has shifted to philanthropy.

As a young boy, he excelled in science and mathematics. His parents recognized his gifts and enrolled him in a private school known for its demanding academic environment. When Bill was 13, he got hooked on computers and surpassed the knowledge of his teacher within a week. Soon he wrote his first computer program. That was the beginning, and he has not deviated from this core focus since. His core task is what brought him prosperity.

Prosperity as I define it, transcends the different types of leaders and the kinds of endeavors they are involved in.

Prosperity for a religious leader is how close he or she is to God, how much he or she serves their Lord. That's what makes them prosper. Political leaders define prosperity as being significant and having an impact on issues that affect society. Prosperity for business leaders is not merely financial gain; they are driven by a desire for creating a greater good.

Our core task in Network Marketing is prospecting. Prospecting is the only thing you get paid to do.

If you want to achieve prosperity in Network Marketing, that requires you focus all your energy on prospecting without distraction.

Anything else will slow your progress in reaching your goals. And if your why is strong enough, this focus will propel you to achieve all you desire, dream of and deserve.

Three Key Reasons

When I first got involved in Network Marketing, prospecting was easy for me. I'd call up a friend and say, "Hey, listen, I got involved in a new business. I want you to take a look at it." Most of the time, they wouldn't look at it. They'd just give me their credit card.

Now I realize that this was not duplicatable, but it did have something to do with credibility, and in all aspects of recruiting, that kind of trust is paramount.

Beyond all the training I received about various systems or how to handle objections, the best advice I ever received about prospecting was from Michael Clouse. I attended a seminar shortly after I began my Network Marketing career where Michael said that people join this business for three reasons:

"They know you, they like you, and they trust you."

Trust is key. You might know someone, and you may like that person, but do you trust that individual?

It's possible to be in business with somebody and trust him or her completely, even if you don't necessarily like them all that much. On the other hand, you may know and like someone a great deal, but when it comes to business you absolutely do not trust them… There's no way you would ever go into business with that person. Trust is key.

Relationship Building

One thing that drives me today is my love of introducing new people to this business. It's all about relationship building, which involves a step-by-step process.

Have you ever had the experience of striking up a conversation with someone at a party with the intent of prospecting them? You eventually hit them with that age-old, traditional introduction line: "Hey, you'd be good in my business," and you follow it with a myriad of statements about how great your product and opportunity is. The person seems interested, so you ask for their phone number, and they give it to you. You think the interaction went great, but when you call back a few days later, they don't answer the phone.

A key distinction here is that your ability to prospect is tied to building relationships, not offending people.

Often when you offend someone, they won't let on that they're offended. When you prospect someone at a party, while they might placate you by listening to what you have to say, the bottom line is that they might be a little bit offended that you'd bring up business at a party. They'll give you their phone number, but that's just an easy way to end an uncomfortable conversation. They have no intention of picking up the phone if you call.

The opposite of offending people is pleasing and delighting them. So, how do you do that? Here's a true story that shows you exactly how:

> A number of years ago one of the editors of Psychology Today magazine was writing a book on human behavior. As part of his research for the book, he bought a first class plane ticket from New York to L.A. with the intention of sitting next to someone and only asking that person questions. He would make no declarative statements, volunteer no information; only ask questions. Sure enough, a man sat down next to him and that's what he did for the six-hour flight across the country.

When the plane landed in L.A. the editor has his assistant interview his seatmate. Two remarkable things came out of the interview. First, the man who sat next to the editor of Psychology Today admitted he didn't know the editor's name. A pretty good indication the editor didn't reveal anything. But the second thing was the amazing part.

This man, who sat next to the editor of Psychology Today who only asked him questions for six hours said, "He was the most interesting person he had ever met in his life!"

The very best way in the world to please and delight people is to be sincerely curious about who and how they are. If you're honest, you'll admit you are your favorite subject and when I'm interested in you, when I ask you about you and what makes you think that or say this or feel that way... you're going to "fall in like" with me right away. That's friendship.

And it doesn't have to take six hours either. You can turn a casual acquaintance into a friendship in three to five minutes by asking questions and being truly interested in the other person. I do it every day.

Three Simple Steps

Since most of your time should be spent prospecting, you want to do it as efficiently as possible. More than 70% of the Network Marketing businesses I've built, I've done on the phone. I've worked from home.

Regardless if I am talking to a stay-at-home mom, a CEO of a company or a blue-collar worker, I always follow the exact same three steps— every single time.

These three steps are:

1. **Call them**

2. **Refer them/meet them**

3. **Follow up with Them**

Imagine that you are pouring each of the prospects on your list into a funnel. Inside the funnel you go through three steps that allow your prospect to systematically review the merits of your opportunity, the owners, the management team, the product you're marketing, the compensation plan, and the timing of your company. At the other end of this systematic review, the prospect emerges as either a "yes," a "no," or a "maybe."

If you do this properly and always focus on the relationship first, you'll produce incredible results.

Prospecting Is a Process

Here is a vital piece of information to always keep in mind:

Prospecting is a process, not an event.

I recently sponsored a woman in my Network Marketing business that I had been prospecting for three-and-a-half years. When I first contacted her from an Internet ad, it simply wasn't the right time in her life. I stayed in touch with her regularly, and finally the time was right for her to join my team.

Prospecting is a process, not an event.

Many people get on the phone and when enough prospects say no, they get frustrated and quit. But I've learned that a lot of the top prospectors in our business never try to finish the deal on the first call. Sometimes it takes years to get somebody into your business and you'll find that those folks tend to stay committed longer and succeed more, too.

Build Friends, Not Income

One of my mentors told me that a millionaire in Network Marketing is defined as someone who has a million friends. If you focus on relationships, the money truly does come— and often, sooner than later.

Many people choose not to join a Network Marketing business because they get offended at some point in the process. It might not be because they don't like the business, although they frequently say that's their reason. I have learned over the years, "The Reason Is Never the Reason." If you can build trust with your prospects, the whole process is so much easier.

One of the easiest ways to offend somebody is to prematurely bring up your business when they are not in a receptive mindset.

I seldom start talking business details unless it's a telephone call that I initiate. This enables me to steer clear of any pitfalls. For instance, at a party, people are there to enjoy themselves. They are not there looking for a business opportunity. When you meet someone that you know would be perfect for the business, you will become overwhelmed by the desire to tell them about your opportunity immediately. Don't do it. In that initial encounter if you focus on building a relationship, you will get the time to tell them about your business in a more controlled setting later.

The Law of Reciprocity

Reciprocity is the give and take of life. It's doing something for somebody else that they will feel compelled to repay.

Let's say you're moving next Saturday. You call me and ask me to help you, and of course I agree (reluctantly) because we're friends even though I hate moving. A few months later, I have to move. Who do you think I'm going to call first? You! And even though it's an inconvenience, you're going to assist me. Why? Because I assisted you. That's reciprocity.

Simple salutations are another example of reciprocity. I see you on the street, I walk up to you, and I say, "Hi, how are you doing today?" Of course, you reply right away, "Great, how are you doing?" Reciprocity is at work around us every day.

In the recruiting process, even though I never mention my opportunity the first time I meet anyone, I've developed a strategy I learned from my mentors. If I focus on getting to know someone first— if I begin to like them and trust them, and if they begin to like and trust me— then, by using the law of reciprocity, I can get their phone number every single time.

My goal in any initial interaction with anyone is to start building a friendship and to obtain a phone number. That's it.

Even if I think they might be a good fit in my business, that's all I'll do. I will not mention my product or my service intentionally.

Something else I never do is to hand out business cards to prospects. I don't even carry them. I use business cards for people in my downline, upline, or crossline that I want to keep in touch with. For my prospects, I only request business cards. I never give them.

Here's a great example...

Let's say I'm introduced to you at a social function. I think, "Wow, this person has a great personality. He/She would be perfect for my business." Instead of bringing up my opportunity, I'll ask you about your family, your occupation, and your hobbies. I'll pay very close attention to what you're saying, and I won't interrupt you.

Eventually I'm going to get you talking about something you really like. There's one common subject that we all like to talk about that brings us incredible joy: Ourselves. I engage my prospects in casual conversation, asking them lots of open-ended questions, and this leads them to willingly give me their phone numbers every time.

At the right point when I know we are having a great talk (I know you are enjoying it as we are talking about you), I'll stop the conversation, simply ask for your phone number, and you'll give it to me.

I'll say something like, "I've really appreciated talking to you. I've got to move on right now, but hey, can I have your phone number? I'd really like to call you back and hear more about your horses. They sound amazing."

You'll be happy to give me your phone number. You'll think, "Wow, I really like Ken. I want to talk to him some more." And you think that because I gave you the chance to speak about your favorite subject and we all enjoy that.

And just because I'm not actually mentioning business at that point, I'm still prospecting. I collect those phone numbers, and then I just pour those people back into my funnel.

What Are the Odds?

What are the odds of somebody you're prospecting joining your downline? One in 10, two in 20, one in 50, one in a 100? Here is my theory:

The odds of getting somebody to join a Network Marketing business are one in 365.

Every person out there that you will ever talk to will join your business— even the most skeptical, negative person— if you get them on the right day. To me, that's the fun part, the most exciting part, of prospecting.

People join a Network Marketing business for many reasons. One person joins because he wants to make more money. Someone else joins because she loves the product. Some folks join because they are looking for something new in their lives. Maybe they're sick and tired of being sick and tired. They're frustrated with their jobs.

One person's reason might not necessarily be the money— it might be that he or she wants a challenge. Maybe an individual is having trouble at home and this will provide something positive to focus on. For others, it's all the negative friends they have and they see all the positive people in Network Marketing and they want to be around them.

Prospecting is a process, not an event. If you agree with my theory that every single person will join on the right day, then it becomes just as important to develop a system for following up properly with people as it is to introduce this business to new people. Both parts of the equation are equally important.

A Game of Chance

Several months ago I was asked to speak at a major event at the Grand Hotel in Kelowna, British Columbia. During the day we had an amazing event with hundreds of people in attendance, and in the evening I visited the hotel casino.

I love people watching. I meandered up to a roulette table, where a group of about 15 people were gathered. Now, for those of you who aren't familiar with roulette, the game is played with a ball and a wheel. On the wheel there are 38 separate pockets around the circumference where the ball can settle in and stop— some are red and some are black, and they're divided equally all around the wheel. And there are two spots that are green; one is labeled zero, and the other one is double zero.

Those playing the game bet on which color and specific number the ball will land on. The croupier spins the wheel, and then takes a little silver ball and spins it the opposite way. As the wheel slows down and the momentum of the ball decreases, the ball drops down into the inner wheel, bounces around crazily between the numbers, and then finally rests in one spot and that's the winner.

I stayed at the roulette table for quite some time, watching the dealer effortlessly spinning that wheel and the ball, over and over again. The ball would stop— he'd start again. The ball would stop again and he'd start again. And then it hit me— I saw a parallel to prospecting.

Let's say that the silver ball is your prospect, and the green zero is the moment they say yes. Think about this:

It doesn't matter how often you speak to them— you want to speak to them in a way that allows you to spin the ball again.

Once you've got somebody into the "like" stage, call them once a month... Imagine that the ball is the prospect, the green zero is a yes, and there's a little more than a month of spaces on that wheel.

If the dealer keeps spinning that ball again, over and over and over, eventually that silver ball will land on the green zero. Eventually the prospect will say yes. You just never know when.

It's the odds of the game— prospecting is a game of chance.

Everybody will join a Network Marketing business, but you don't know when. You just have to keep spinning the ball... you just have to keep contacting them. You want to create a system, just like the dealer has spinning that ball again and again.

Increase Your Odds

In the game of roulette, if there's one silver ball and forty places for it to stop, how do you get it to stop on the green zero more often? You're probably thinking, "Spin it more often." Okay...

Now, I want you to change that mindset. The real answer is: "Add more balls."

Imagine that there are forty-two silver balls. Every time you spin the wheel, what happens? A prospect would join just about every single time the balls stopped. Wouldn't that be much easier?

Prospecting is very much like that. Someone is going to say yes every time. Remember, your chances of getting somebody to join are one in 365. They will join when it is the right day for them and you won't know unless you stay in touch. The question is: Do you have the focus and fortitude to stick with it?

I did— I learned early on that if I just kept talking to people, focusing on getting to know them, like them, trust them and vice versa, the rest would happen on its own. Just like the game of roulette, I learned to develop a system that would allow me to keep spinning the balls every day.

Your Master List

My system starts with a master list. I created my master list on Day One in the business, and I do it again once each year. I write down every single person I meet.

If this book has caused you to re-examine your methods for working your business and you want to reach for more, then remember that every day can be a new day in Network Marketing. Once you've finished reading this, make it day one in Network Marketing for you. Don't wait for the end of the book. Read about prospecting and defining your core task and get to work.

Create a list of each and every person you've ever met in your life. This might sound trite to you— it sounded corny to me when someone, who happened to be a millionaire, first told me to do this. I didn't understand the importance of it at first, but after a couple of months when I started to get frustrated because things weren't working for me, I decided to write that list.

In the beginning, I just called my friends and said, "Hey, Joe, I just got started with this brand-new business. We're going to make a ton of money. The buy-in is $2,400. Give me your credit card."

While I did have some initial success in getting people to join my business, after a couple of months my income wasn't going up as fast as I would have imagined, and some of my initial reps became frustrated and quit. That's when I realized how important systems were.

I realized that how *you* prospect somebody is how you're training *your prospect* to prospect somebody.

How *you* sponsor somebody into this business is the way *they'll* sponsor someone.

I might be able to sign someone up by just asking for his credit card, but the average person can't do that.

Success in Network Marketing requires following a simple system from day one. Creating your master list is the first step.

Begin by writing down every person you've ever met in your life. Get out your old high school yearbooks. Don't worry about phone numbers at this point. Use the phone book as a memory jogger. The average person over the age of 20 has met more than 2,000 people, so your list should consist of hundreds of people.

Once you've compiled your master list, make another list of 50 or 60 people that have similar desirable characteristics. You are looking for the qualities that top income earners in Network Marketing all seem to share. I call this creating your "dream team."

The Qualities of Top Income Earners

1. They are hard workers.

2. They are honest.

3. They smile easily.

4. They are positive and upbeat.

5. They have incredible drive and motivation.

6. They stand out in a crowd.

Select people from your master list as if you were putting together an NBA finals basketball team or a Stanley Cup-winning hockey team. These are the people you want to start with.

Now, begin putting this group of people through the funnel.

Step one is initiating a phone call. Give them a call to rekindle or revitalize your relationship. My phone calls sound like this:

> *"Hey, Dan, I'm just giving you a call because I was thinking about you. I got involved in a new business that I want to share with you. How are you doing today?"*

I introduce the reason I'm calling them, and then I change the subject as quickly as possible back to... **them!**

Remember, we all enjoy talking about ourselves. I get them chatting about what's going on, and I make it fun and light. And I always remember to SMILE when I'm on the phone— it really makes a huge difference. No kidding.

I just read a post by Ron Gutman, founder and CEO of HealthTap, about the power of a smile. He told about a UC Berkeley 30-year study that examined the smiles of students in an old yearbook, and measured their well-being and success throughout their lives. By measuring the smiles in the photographs the researchers were able to predict: How fulfilling and long-lasting their marriages would be, how highly they would score on standardized tests of well-being and general happiness, and how inspiring they would be to others. The widest smilers consistently ranked highest in all of the above.

Even more surprising, Gutman pointed out, was a 2010 Wayne State University research project that examined the baseball cards photos of Major League players in 1952. The study found that the span of a player's smile could actually predict the span of his life! Players who didn't smile in their pictures lived an average of only 72.9 years, while players with beaming smiles lived an average of 79.9 years.

Then the post reported about a fascinating study conducted in Great Britain where researchers found that one smile can provide the same level of measurable brain stimulation as up to 2,000 chocolate bars! They also found that smiling can be as stimulating as receiving up to 16,000 Pounds Sterling in cash. (That's 25 grand ($US) per smile.)

The author humorously pointed out that unlike lots of chocolate, lots of smiling can actually make you healthier. He wrote "...smiling has documented therapeutic effects, and has been associated with reduced stress hormone levels (like cortisol, adrenaline, and dopamine), increased health and mood enhancing hormone levels (like endorphins), and lowered blood pressure."

There's more: A recent Penn State University study confirmed that when we smile we not only appear more likeable and courteous, but we're actually perceived to be more *competent*.

And what came next really made me smile (and you'll immediately know why):

"Perhaps this is why," the author concluded, "Mother Teresa said: 'I will never understand all the good that a simple smile can accomplish.'"

I've always appreciated the power of a smile. Now, after reading this scientific material, I know why.

So, during this initial conversation, never interrupt them in the middle of a sentence, no matter what. Engage their heart as well as their head by asking them questions. Let them talk about things that matter to them. You can use the FORM method (asking about their Family, Occupation, Recreation, and Mission) to find the right questions. This is such an easy philosophy to follow on the phone.

Your conversation might last 10 or 15 minutes, and then at some point the other person will pause. This means he or she is satisfied. Now you can say...

"Hey, listen, John. I really have to tell you about this business. It's amazing. I'd really like your opinion on it. Can you take a look at something for me?"

This is where reciprocity kicks in. When they say, "Yes, of course," you can send them to your company's Web site, and then you can simply book an appointment to follow up with them.

If they're in your local area, you can say...

"John, I want to get together and go over this with you after you've looked at the Web site. When do you have time for a coffee in the next couple of days?"

John will agree because you've used reciprocity. Get a date booked right there on that first call. If it's a long-distance situation, you can say...

"I want to call you back in a couple days. I'm available Thursday through Saturday between 5:00 and 8:00. Just give me a time that works for you."

And then remember to be prompt and punctual when you do call them back.

You'll notice that 90% of the call was about the prospect. You directed them to a Web site, and you booked an appointment. You didn't mention your product, or the compensation plan, or the owners of the company; instead, you focused *on them,* and you pointed them to a presentation.

As one of my mentors taught me, "In Network Marketing, if you're doing it right, when you open your mouth, you should be pointing at a tool."

Elite prospectors are good traffic cops. They direct people to sources of information.

The same process works with your "cold" prospects. When you've met someone socially and have come away with his or her phone number, you let a short amount of time elapse and then you call that person back. You can say...

> *"Hey, Sue, I'm giving you a call. We met last Monday night at the party. You were telling me about your saber-toothed tiger. Do you remember me?"*

Right away in Sue's mind, she's thinking, "Oh, talking with him was great. He was so curious about me. I'm so happy to hear from him." From there you can go into the same process as calling your warm market prospects.

After you talk about her interests for a few minutes and there's an appropriate pause, you can then say...

> *"Hey, Sue, listen, I've gotten involved in a business recently, (or "I've been involved in a business for a while"), and your personality is the same as some of the most successful people I work with. I'd love your opinion. Can you do me a favor and take a look at this business for me? It just involves looking at a Web site."*

Of course she'll say yes.

Contrast this to those times when you have a sense that someone would be great in your business, but when you call them back, you're never able to reach them, or they never call you back. They're thinking, "Oh yeah, there's that Network Marketing guy. He wants to get me involved in a pyramid." But if you follow this strategy, you'll never have that happen again.

So what happens next? You meet for your scheduled appointment either on the phone or in person a few days later. Always make it a few days later; this gives you time to hook up with somebody else who you can bring with you to the appointment or have available by phone.

The Follow-Up Appointment

After you build some rapport with your prospect, you ask them...

"So, what did you think of the Web site?"

Nine out of 10 of the individuals you prospect in your business will not have looked at the Web site. But that's okay. It doesn't really matter. You're expecting this. You say next,

"I've arranged for Ken, one of my business partners, to speak with you. Hold on for a second."

Bring Ken on the call and say...

"Hey, Ken, I've got John here. He's a really amazing guy."

Openly compliment your prospect— this strokes his or her ego in a good way. Yes, you have to mean it. Seriously— if you don't like people, don't join a Network Marketing business. Be sincere and mean what you say. The bottom line is that you must always take your prospects seriously.

Remember things about them. Take notes on them. Truly have a desire to be their friend, and your prospecting will go through the roof.

Introducing your upline enables another person to answer all of your prospect's questions, go over the details of the business, and bring them to a logical conclusion. Your job is simply to direct your prospect to the information and then get somebody else to fill in the gaps.

Why do I stress this?

I could give you as great an explanation about our product as anybody. I can talk about the company owners as well as anybody. But I don't do it, because the person I'm prospecting can't do it. Later on, I want to be able to say to them, "Listen, Erica. You can do this. Look how easy it is. Look at me. I didn't even mention the business to you." This is true duplication.

The Point of Logical Conclusion

By the end of the conversation, your prospect will have reached a logical conclusion. They can conclude one of three things:

1. **"Yes, I like this business. I'm ready to join."**

2. **"Maybe... I'm not sure. Maybe I'll try the product."**

3. **"No, I'm not interested."**

If they say yes, you literally spin them around— you take them from the narrow end of the funnel and put them right at the top of the funnel again. Now they begin to build their list, introduce the business to their friends, and utilize the same three-step process: The initial call, the invitation to view a Web site, and a follow-up meeting on the phone or in person. And you just keep repeating this process.

Once you've built that list, keep it going.

You're going to be attending meetings. You're going to be in society. You're going to get busy in life. The greatest prospectors in the world are *out in the world,* always meeting new people. Plan to attend some networking events. Get to know more people. Just get out there where the people are. If you increase your exposure to the world, you're going to increase your list of prospects.

When I changed my strategy and started using this process, everybody I brought onto my team began to do the same thing. I used the people above me for third-party validation, and the people I brought in used me. Everything started falling into place, and my checks started increasing.

Handling the Nos

What do you do when somebody says no? Call that person once a month, just to say hello. If you contact that person once a month, you will have incredible success in Network Marketing, even if they continue to say no. And if you've done this the right way, you'll never have to worry about anybody being offended by the process.

Out of all the people that have said no to me, at least 50% of them eventually said yes to me.

The first time I called my friend Mitzi in Florida three-and-a-half years ago, she said no to me. I called her the next month and didn't even mention my business. I just followed up with her every single month, just to say hello.

Of course, I was taking great notes on what was going on in our conversations so I'd remember a couple of little points to bring up. I'd just say…

> *"Hey, Mitzi, I'm checking in. I've really appreciated building a friendship with you, and I want to keep that friendship going. How are you doing? How's it going with your son's hockey obsession?"*

But when you call, remember that you are just building a friendship. Call once a month until the day you catch them on the right day. Remember that roulette wheel— you don't know when the ball is going to hit that green zero. You might spin that wheel a hundred times before it hits the green zero, but it *will* eventually hit the green zero.

Repetition

Focus on just using the same system over and over again. Call your prospects once a month. You'll get so many people into your funnel that it's going to be hard to communicate with them all on a monthly basis. You can use e-cards, or you can send them a brief little email. And every two months or so when you're talking to them, you can say, "Hey, listen, my business is still going great. Are you in a different space right now?" Just listen to what they say.

What happened with Mitzi is that one month when I called her, her family was moving from Gainesville to Tampa Bay, and she was open to the idea of a new business. The timing was perfect, and she ended up joining me.

Handling Objections Equals Losing Friends

One of my pet peeves in this industry is "handling objections." It's something I never, ever do.

Now, don't get me wrong— if somebody has a question about the business or they need clarification on something, I'm happy to answer them.

Handling objections is a science that's sometimes taught in our industry. What it really means is you've got a silver tongue and can spin it around a ball and tie a double-half-twisted-loop knot in the back and you're going get somebody to join every single time.

Let's say you're leading a prospect through the process, and, after taking a look at the business, they say, "No thanks, I'm not interested." They go on to say that it sounds too much like a pyramid. You tell them, "Well, our government is a true pyramid. The president's at the top, the vice president is below him, and everybody else is below there, and it all works well." While this might be clever (and even true), you're contradicting their mindset.

Or somebody might say to you, "Oh, I don't have the time." One age-old classic answer to this objection is, "Well, you don't need the time. Busy people get things done." What you have to realize is that all of those excuses aren't the real reasons why they aren't joining.

The real reason they decided not to join is that it just wasn't the right day.

Just keep spinning the wheel!

If you want to be able to call that person month after month and continue building a friendship, don't handle objections. Instead, say to the person, "Listen, I really appreciate you looking at this for me. Your friendship is more important to me than making money, so let's just leave it at that." Then continue your conversation.

If you want to prod the person a little bit, you might say, "Would you mind telling me why?" or "Is there anything that I missed in my explanation to you that could assist you?" But if they give you a straight-out objection, you make the decision to either "handle an objection" at the risk of losing friends, or just continue to build the friendship.

Here's an example.

Let's say you have a specific opinion on a matter, and I have the opposite opinion. In our conversation, I oppose your opinion and I become adamant about my views. I handle your objection, or I contradict your belief. If somebody has a belief or opinion and you contradict it, how conducive is that to making friends? If I'm prospecting you, and you've got a different opinion and I contradict it, are you going to like me? Absolutely not!

Handling objections might be great for those salespeople who can sell ice to an Eskimo, but the average person isn't like that. If we can teach average people to build friendships, it keeps giving them a chance to roll that ball around the wheel over and over again by just calling their prospects once a month.

The key is to stay in touch regularly. This provides more and more chances to contact them on the right day.

Use a little spreadsheet to keep track of your calls so you know when to call your prospects, or create a reminder in your agenda or PDA to keep you on track. You'll be surprised at how much your prospecting results will increase.

Honor people and build friendships, and they'll sign up when it's the right day for them. This is really what the term "service to others" means. It's all about trust, respect, and partnership.

The Truth about Duplication

During my first couple of years in Network Marketing, I managed to master the whole area of recruiting, and I had a lot of success. Yet it has always frustrated me that in spite of my best attempts to assist people to recruit the right way, the amount of people that become successful prospectors and recruiters has been miniscule.

My mentors always told me that some people just aren't cut out for being successful recruiters. My mentors felt that many people aren't willing to look in the mirror, they're not willing to be coachable, or their "why" isn't big enough... but I couldn't buy into any of that. What about being able to duplicate— what about having a duplicatable system?

In my own recruiting, I've always done two basic things.

The first one is that I go online and search the Internet for leads. I'll go to Google and target a specific city. Then I'll type in the phrase, "mortgage brokers LA" or "real estate agents LA." This is how I generate leads, and then I'll just call them and ask them if they'd like to take a look at a business.

The second thing I do is that wherever I go locally, I collect business cards from bulletin boards or the fish bowl at a restaurant or a hotel. I call those people and say, "Hey, I got your business card from the restaurant at the hotel," and then ask them if they are open to looking at a business. These two prospecting techniques have worked extremely well for me.

But one day during a training I was conducting for 30 or 40 of my reps, I found myself wondering why, although I thought my approach was duplicatable, I wasn't actually duplicating. As I was speaking, I suddenly stopped in mid-sentence. I had just finished saying, "You know, this whole thing is really duplicatable," and then I stopped and said, "You know what? It's not." I had an "Aha!" moment:

Recruiting and prospecting skills are *not* duplicatable.

Here's the problem: Most leaders in Network Marketing train based on what *they* do. An Internet recruiter trains people how to recruit on the Internet. The relationship-based recruiter trains people how to build relationships. And they all say that their systems are duplicatable.

Procurement and Processing

I really believe that the biggest reason so many people don't do well in this industry is that they do not understand this key point: Prospecting is not an event; it's a sequence of events. There are two main parts to prospecting: one is *procurement* and the other is *processing*.

Procurement means to gather, to collect, to get things organized, to obtain. Procurement is the lead generation side of prospecting:

How do you find the people?

The other side of the equation is processing:

What do you do with those leads?

Here's the difference: There is a duplicatable side to our business. You have to be duplicatable, but only one of the two parts can be duplicated— the processing side. Procurement, the lead generation side, is individualistic in nature.

The way I generate leads works well for me, but what if it doesn't fit your personality? What if I just forget about you because I don't think you can do it, but in actuality the only problem is that you've never found a way to generate leads that fits your style? But what if we just allow people to be free and to individualize how they generate leads? Once someone has generated some leads, then they can learn to duplicate the processing side of it.

We've already covered the processing side of prospecting. You put leads through the three-step process (the funnel) and they come out a "yes," a "no," or a "maybe." It's the procurement side that is tied to your personality.

Ever since I realized this, I've shared the 12 most popular ways to generate leads with my new people. I always start everybody the same way: I get them going in the business, they create a master list, and I do an in-home meeting.

You start processing through the people you know— that's duplicatable.

But I don't know of anyone who has earned a seven figure annual income in this industry based *only* on the people that they know.

This makes the procurement side extremely essential.

I like to share the top 12 ways to generate leads in this business with my new reps. I give them the basics and then ask them which one they'd like to try first. My theory is that everyone can find one or two ways to generate leads that are comfortable for them. (You'll find a list of the twelve ways to generate leads at the end of this chapter.)

Automate the Core Task

Automating the core task is essential if you're going to be a master Network Marketing prospector and recruiter. Even though I struggled with personality issues in the early days, prospecting was second nature to me— it was automatic.

One of the essential qualities of great leaders in our industry is that they've learned to automate the core task of prospecting.

If you were to do a study of the world's great leadership teachers and coaches, trying to pin-point the commonalities, you would find that every single one of them talks about

111

habits. In many of his books, Leadership Guru John C. Maxwell says that is takes 21 days to create a habit. For many people entering the profession, prospecting is brand new. It is crucial to take the advice of Mr. Maxwell, and many others. To truly create walk-away income, you have to make prospecting routine. It is essential to develop the habit of prospecting.

One of the most important elements of prospecting is procurement. If you can find a couple ways to generate leads that you just do naturally, the whole business will become easier for you. Then anytime you're out locally, you've already identified the easiest ways for you to prospect, and you can do it spontaneously.

But what if you can't identify with the way your upline is recruiting? How will you ever become successful? Don't worry, you just haven't found your groove. Remember, the procurement side is individualistic in nature. Your unique personality has to connect with the right lead generation technique.

When I work with a new person now, I run them through the basics of connecting with their warm market, and then instead of saying, "Hey, try collecting business cards," I say, "Okay, this next part is individualistic in nature. That means it's got to fit your personality, so I'm not going to jam something down your throat. Let's start with these 12 options... let's experiment with them a little bit and see what we can come up with that fits your unique personality."

I believe that more people would have been successful in this industry over the years if somebody explained to them that only part of the prospecting process is duplicatable. The most important part is *not* duplicatable.

You have to find something that fits *your* personality.

That's what happened to me. In the very beginning, I found a couple of ways to generate leads that were tied to who I was and felt completely comfortable, and this allowed the whole process to become automatic for me.

Inspired Actions

Find Your Zone

As you read what I just wrote, I hope that you experience a tangible sense of relief. When you realize that you can find ways to generate leads that you're comfortable with, ways that truly work for you, your business starts to become fun!

This is all about getting into your zone with procurement. You can duplicate the three-step process exactly, but until you are comfortable with procurement, you won't be in the zone to process properly. All along, I think we've focused on the wrong roadblock.

It's not that people don't want to follow the three-step process.

It's simply that they haven't found a way to generate leads that fits their personality.

Once you get into your zone, you'll find it much easier to stay focused on your core task— prospecting!

Inspired Actions

12 Ways to Generate Leads

1. Internet search engines (Google, Yahoo, Bing, etc.)

2. Buying leads

3. Collecting business cards

4. Print advertising (newspapers, flyers, local journals)

5. Online advertising

6. Referrals

7. Car ads (advertising, wrapping)

8. Email blasting

9. Social networking (Facebook, Myspace, LinkedIn, etc.)

10. Specialty programs

11. Local social and community groups

12. Extended friends

6

Have a "Why That Makes You Cry

"You must remain focused on your journey to greatness."

LES BROWN

I've always been extremely laser-focused on success, because I've never forgotten what my childhood was like. The biggest driving factor and motivator in my life today is making sure my kids don't ever experience that.

The reason I stay focused is that my "Why" is bigger than anything in my life.

Even now, I can't think about my own upbringing and how much I don't want my kids to go through what I experienced without getting emotional.

You might be able make $10,000 a month in income without an insurmountable "why," but it will be very hard to earn $100,000 a month unless you have a reason buried deep within you that drives you to make this happen. Do yourself a favor: Have more than one— have several. I have two that drive me every single day.

One of the things that I found amazing about the inspirational leaders that I studied is that they all have huge "Whys." If you dig into their lives, you will see that for yourself. I would challenge you to use Google to look into Warren Buffett, Steve Jobs, Bill Gates, or John F. Kennedy, and discover for yourself what drives them.

Powerful Examples

I'll give you a really quick example of how powerful a "Why" can be. Let me paint a picture for you.

Imagine you are walking downtown on your way to an appointment. You're on your way to a restaurant to meet your college-age son, and you have just enough time to get there.

Now, as you round the corner, you come upon absolute mayhem. All you can see is emergency vehicles and people scattered everywhere. There's been a head-on collision in the middle of the road, and you are shocked because you can see a pair of legs pinned underneath the front tire of one of the cars. You stand there with everyone else, and you say, "What's going on here?"

Someone replies, "Oh, gosh, this guy was crossing the road, and these cars, man, boom! The fire trucks are coming right now." And everybody says, "Okay, they'll get him out. He's probably dead anyway."

Suddenly you think, *Oh, I'd better go find my son.* You want to see that he's there. You run to the restaurant (he should be there by now), but you can't find him.

You run back to the accident scene and take a second look, and out of the corner of your eye, you recognize your son's shoes! What happens next?

You are overcome by instant terror. Imagine that right now… Can you feel the knot in your throat as you read this?

Like a flash of light, in the blink of an eye you are over by the car, lifting with all your strength. You manage to lift the car a foot off the ground just as the fire department arrives and the vehicle is removed from the lifeless body.

As the car is removed, you realize that it is not your son! Instantly you are overcome with emotion, and you stand back against a nearby wall to collect yourself. Just as you regain your composure, your son appears and gives you a big hug, almost as if he realized what has just happened to you.

If your reason is strong enough, you can do anything you put your mind to.

It has been proven again and again throughout the ages that human beings can sustain incredible pain and accomplish unbelievable tasks if the reason "Why" is big enough. I have told this story many times in front of crowds as large as ten thousand to illustrate what someone can do if their reason for doing it is big enough.

Imagine standing on top of one of the old World Trade Centers in New York. Picture that. Can you feel it?

You're standing up there in the midst of gale force winds as the towers sway back and forth in the breeze beneath your feet. Did you know that the trade center buildings used to sway between four-to-eight feet, depending on the strength of the wind? They were designed to do that.

Now imagine that there is a steel I-beam (the type used in building construction) stretched between the two buildings right over the New York streets. The I-beam is about four inches wide. Can you picture it?

The wind is blowing... the buildings are swaying, and the beam is floating as it sits there.

Now imagine that you are on one building at the edge of the I-beam, and there is a man standing on the opposite building at the other end of the beam. The man tells you that he will pay you $10,000 to walk across the beam. Would you do it? Obviously not! One wrong step, one gust of wind, and you're gone.

But what if the man offered you $100,000 to cross the beam? Would you do it then?

Now, what if the man was standing on the other tower, the wind blowing so hard that it made your hair stand up, and he was holding one of your children over the edge of the tower. As he dangled your child with one hand, he yelled at you, "Cross the beam right now, or I'll drop your child!"

Obviously, every parent reading this would be halfway across that beam before the man finished his sentence.

It is amazing what can be accomplished when the reason is strong enough.

There are countless examples out there about what people have done in the face of adversity, when their "Why" was big enough. What would you be willing to do for your children, your spouse, or your parents?

I am sure that some of you read the last couple of stories very skeptically. There is always going to be someone that just won't believe. I was one of those people.

During my fifteen years of policing, I was one of the most skeptical people in the world. I was very jaded and dark-humored. At the same time, I was constantly amazed at what people would do if their reason was strong enough.

He Ripped a Car Door Off with His Bare Hands...

I'm writing this chapter during a sixteen-hour flight from Singapore to Los Angeles, and I just recalled a story that illustrates extreme human ability in the face of adversity.

In May of 2000, I was living in Borden, Ontario for a couple of months while I took a policing course. My family was living over 18 hours away in Halifax, Nova Scotia. On the long May weekend that year, my partner Mark and I decided that we would drive to Halifax and surprise our families with a weekend visit. It would be a painfully long trip, but we would share the driving time in order to travel nonstop.

At about 4:00 pm, we were driving along Canada's busiest throughway, Highway 401 just outside of Kingston, Ontario. The rock music on the radio played loudly as we headed for home. Mark was driving and I was drifting off to sleep in the passenger seat.

Just as I was zoning out, Mark hit the brakes hard and yelled, "Holy cow!" I looked up just in time to see an eighteen-wheeler jack-knife into the oncoming traffic, hit six cars, and then head into the ditch that divided the east and westbound lanes.

The ditch was about six feet lower than the surface of the road. Even though the big rig was now on its side, it hit the ditch doing at least forty miles an hour. Because of the lower grade, when the truck came out of the ditch into our lane, it was launched into the air.

I remember this event like it was happening again right before my eyes. What happened in seconds comes back to me in minutes. I watched the truck as if in slow motion.

Four p.m. on the Friday of a long weekend meant that the highway was jam-packed. That rig (that was hauling steel) came back to the road, landed on another seven cars before sliding to a stop in an adjacent field. The resulting scene was apocalyptic. Immediately our police training kicked in and Mark and I jumped out of the car and ran to the scene.

Along with several other Good Samaritans, we spent the next three hours tending to the injured. It was horrific. To this date, it is still the worst accident ever to occur on the 401. Many people lost their lives that day.

After everything calmed down, a police officer took a statement from me for his records. As I recounted what had occurred and my observations, he walked me through the scene so I could point things out to him as we spoke.

I told the officer how I approached one of the cars that the rig had landed on and found a woman unconscious in the passenger seat with massive injuries. I attempted to locate a pulse and realized that there was none. Due to the recent timing of the accident, Mark and I made a decision to remove the woman from the car and begin CPR.

As I was explaining how we set the woman on the ground, the officer interrupted me and asked me where we got the "jaws of life" (a powerful mechanical air

121

compression tool used to rip cars apart in accident situations). I told him we didn't have that tool. He asked, "Well, how did you remove the car door?"

I looked over at the door, shocked. Another of the Samaritans who was standing beside us interjected, "You guys just ripped the door off— don't you remember?" My jaw dropped. I had no recollection of ripping the door off that car.

While the observer explained to the police officer, Mark confirmed that we had ripped the door of the car off. He explained that because the door had been badly damaged, we couldn't get it open, and so we tore it off. I was so intensely focused on starting CPR on the victim I didn't realize what we had done. Our adrenaline was running so high and fast through our bodies in the middle of this crisis situation we were able to accomplish a normally impossible, truly superhuman task.

Focus on Your Passion

Warren Buffett is an extraordinary example of someone who knows his "Why" and has accomplished great success because of it. He knew what he wanted and how to get there from a very young age.

Even as a child, Buffett's prized possession was a coin-changer, and when his father offered to take him on a trip, young Warren chose the New York Stock Exchange as his destination. Not long after this, he read a book called *One Thousand Ways to Make $1,000,* and he told his friends he planned to be a millionaire by the time he was 35. Remember, this was back in the tough economic times of 1941, but Buffett was sure he could achieve this.

Buffett himself has said that he attributes his success to focus.

In the book *Snowball: Warren Buffett and the Business of Life* by Alice Schroeder (the title comes from Buffett's advice on success: Find some wet snow and a really long hill), the author says, "He ruled out paying attention to almost anything but business— art, literature, science, travel, architecture— so that he could focus on his passion." Warren Buffett has a empowering "Why" and a powerful focus— so much so that when you hear his name, you immediately think of "great wealth and investing."

My Own "Why"

I've shared the story of my early days with you. To this day, I vividly recall those feelings from over 25 years ago. Wanting something different for myself and my family still propels me forward. In his classic book, *Think and Grow Rich*, Napoleon Hill calls it "Burning Desire." It's definitely a "Why" that makes me cry!

My Dad Gives Me Strength

I am the son of a naval officer. My dad served in the Canadian Navy his entire adult life, over 37 years. In 2006, my dad lost his life to a vicious disease called ALS (Lou Gehrig's disease). This is the most pathetic, undiscriminating disease known to man.

Prior to contracting ALS, my dad was one of the healthiest people that I knew. In 2005, Dad got a cold that never went away. After a couple of months, he went to the hospital for a checkup and was diagnosed with ALS. His health deteriorated quickly after that.

I was sitting in the room with my mom and dad when his doctor delivered the news. The doctor said, "He has only a few months to live." Just writing these words has caused me to tremble.

Just over a year later, I sat beside my dad's hospital bed. The disease had robbed him of his body. He was 140 pounds lighter, and he had lost the ability to speak, to use his hands and legs, or to communicate in any way. The pain he experienced was out of control. My dad passed away that night at 54 years old. It's not fair. He didn't deserve that.

In my 15 years of police work, I knew bad people who deserved something like that, but my dad didn't. So far, no one knows what causes ALS. Now I try to live the healthiest life possible in his honor.

You Will Make Sacrifices Along the Way...

By the time my flight lands in Los Angeles, I will have traveled over 180,000 miles on airplanes this year. I will have spent over 100 nights in hotels. I am saddened to say this, but I just missed my son Matthew's first piano recital last weekend while I was in Jakarta, Indonesia. I have missed birthdays, anniversaries, and many other special occasions while I have been traveling the world building my business.

I can't watch movies on the plane that have kids in them without crying, because of how much I miss Laura, Matthew and Julie when I'm away.

You need to know that the greatness you achieve will involve sacrifices. Your "Why" has to be strong enough to endure the pain.

Believe me, it is easier to give up, but what would that cause?

Personally, I cannot give up. My "Whys" are too important! I NEVER want my children to live the life that I lived growing up, and I don't want their children to live that life either. Don't get me wrong! When I get home tonight, it is going to be complete family time. We'll do our best to make up for the time that I was away.

Discover Your Own "Why"

Your ability to succeed in achieving your desired success is directly related to your awareness of why you want that success. These underlying reasons, beliefs, and values form your core motivation. They are the driving force to ultimately release your potential and personality.

Basically, your attitudes and your zeal to succeed are the external expression of what's going on internally with you— strong emotions that may have evolved out of hurt, needs, or aspirations.

It's important to write out your "Why." Dig deep within yourself to discover your own reasons for pursuing success.

- Why did you get into Network Marketing in the first place?

- What made you want to start your own business?

- Is it because you wanted to be your own boss?

- Did you want more freedom?

- More time to spend with your family?

- More money?

125

Whatever your "Why" is, that's what will keep you going when things aren't going as well as you want.

Once you have your "Why" down in writing, read it— out loud— every day.

Read it when you wake up in the morning and again in the evening before going to sleep.

Doing this on a daily basis will assist you to cement your "Why" deep down in your heart and mind. You might even choose to write out your "Why" every morning, changing it, making it bigger and better. This can really keep you focused, and keep your mind open for new opportunities throughout the day. It is unbelievable what this activity can do for your daily motivation, because it will move you to inspired action.

Don't keep your "Why" to yourself, either. Sharing your "Why" with others sends your convictions into overdrive! This will propel you into massive action, and your powerful behavior will supercharge others too.

Inspired Actions

Hints on Finding Your Real "Why"

1. Your "Why" should make your cry.

2. Look back through your life, reflecting on everything.

3. Be ready— your "Why" may come to you when you're least expecting it!

4. Determine the one thing that causes you the most stress today, that brings tears to your eyes— the one thing that will be gone once you create success in Network Marketing.

5. Your "Why" is the reason you keep going even when you want to quit.

7

Improve Your Communication

*"Effective communication is 20% what you know
and 80% how you feel about what you know."*

JIM ROHN

If you've ever seen Steve Jobs give a keynote address, you'll undoubtedly agree that he's one of the most extraordinary speakers in corporate America. Jobs learned a long time ago that a leader must be part evangelist and part brand spokesperson.

I think Steve Jobs is magnificent to watch. What makes his presentations so dazzling is he does not sell bits of metal, plastic or even advanced technology. He sells a user experience. Instead of focusing on mind-numbing statistics, he sells the advantages and benefits his customers want and will enjoy. When introducing a new Apple product, he clearly explains what it means to the consumer.

He reviews and rehearses all of his presentations.

That sense of casual informality that he portrays only comes after hours and hours *and hours* of practice.

Jobs has an infectious enthusiasm. He exudes passion and energy. And there's no better example of this passion than the famous story of how he convinced John Sculley to lead Apple

Computer in the mid '80s by asking him, "Do you want to sell sugared water all your life or do you want to change the world?" The former Pepsi executive chose the latter, and although their partnership ultimately failed, it reflects Jobs' sense of mission— a mission that he communicated consistently in the early years of Apple and still communicates today.

In my own life, I had no choice but to become a communicator. Ever since I was 18 years old, I've had to collect "the facts" and learn to assemble those facts in a way that made sense, that was clear and compelling and then I learned to present them in a way that would persuade people.

Over the course of my 15 years in police work, I must have testified in court thousands of times. I had to learn how to get my point across in a way that communicated all the details succinctly. I discovered how to be very accurate in a short amount of time.

Think for a second about someone you know that is extremely successful. I'll bet they're great speakers, too. Their ability to speak is likely to be pretty captivating.

When I studied that amazing group of seven leaders, I was not surprised to learn that all were great speakers.

It is essential to be a great communicator if you want to be a great success.

It's vital that you are understood, powerful and influential. And I truly believe that anyone can become a great speaker if he or she really works at it.

If you want to be extremely successful in Network Marketing, it will be easier if you can communicate well. Don't get me wrong— you can become successful even if you are not a good speaker, but it will take longer and be a more difficult.

Be Detailed, but Don't Over-Communicate

Many people over-explain things, and I was no exception. In court, I always knew when I'd gone too far when I'd see the judge's eyes glaze over, and I'd realize that he was tuned out to what I was trying to explain. I wanted so desperately for the judge to really understand what I was saying that often I'd repeat myself six or seven times in the process, which was *not* effective.

To effectively communicate with someone, communicate the details, then stop after you've said something the first time.

I can't tell you the number of people that I've met who start talking and just keep talking not even realizing that they are repeating themselves.

This is called over-communicating.

Instead, be cognizant of the fact that you only have to tell your story once. Communicate the details concisely and clearly the first time and you will be understood.

I've noticed two main reasons people become trapped in over-communication:

1. First; they feel they need to say things several times in order to get their point across…

2. Second; they just don't realize that it is happening.

No matter what the reason, over-communicating is as bad, perhaps even worse, than under-communicating.

But the wonderful thing is that you can identify if you have developed this habit.

Try this technique:

Choose a subject that you like to talk about. Now find a recording device and record yourself talking. Find someone to explain it to and do that. It is very easy to realize if you are over talking when you play back the recording.

How you say things is just as important as *what* you say. If you become skilled at how you say things, you won't have to repeat yourself over and over again. I encourage you to practice this.

If you are someone who oversells a point, then begin to do things differently. For instance, intentionally stop after you've said something the first time. That will be uncomfortable for you in the beginning, but you'll get good at it pretty quickly and it will become second nature to you.

Do you know someone who talks so much that it becomes painful? Even the mere thought of this person causes you to wince.

I know several people that just talk way too much. I'd like to just reach out and tell them, but unfortunately those people would be offended to hear me say this, so hopefully they'll read this book. In the past, I have actually told some people that they talk too much, but it never seems to come across right. This is a sensitive topic, but people who talk too much are hurting themselves.

When you have spoken clearly and concisely, how do you know if someone has really understood what you've said? Just ask.

This way, the other person directly experiences your commitment to communicating and the care and consideration you have for them. And, you'll know if a certain point requires more clarification or information.

Use Stories to Communicate

One thing I observed in all of my mentors is that they speak in stories. Whenever they would try and get a point across to me, they would share related experiences and tell a story around the point.

Instead of just telling me to go in a certain direction or do something, they would share a story about a related experience, a story about themselves or someone they knew.

"You know, I have a friend that went through that exact situation." (Explain the story next and then share what your friend inevitably did).

You might think that it's awkward to speak that way, or that it would be easier to just get to the point. That's what I thought too, and the way I communicated in my first year in Network Marketing was always curt and to the point. And you already know what that got me: A charter membership in the NFL (No Friends Left) Society!

By the way, the power of telling a story isn't just my experience, or the way the Inspirational Leaders I studied preferred to communicate and teach. It's a scientific fact – if you want to be a powerful communicator, read the best-selling book *Influencer: The Power to Change Anything*. You'll learn first-hand "Why" and how stories are the most successful form of verbal persuasion.

How I Became an Effective Communicator

I barely got out of high school. I'm pretty sure that I only graduated because one of my teachers felt pity for me. Obviously, I never went to university.

Literature was never my strong suit, but because I spent fifteen years in policing, every day I collected details and I had to communicate those details to a judge or a jury so that they could understand them.

It was essential that I developed the skill of effectively communicating so a judge felt that I truly knew what I was talking about and believed me. Taking the oath before testifying was no guarantee that a particular judge would find me credible.

Thousands of hours giving evidence, watching juries and judges, I realized that they responded as much to the tone I used and the way I said things as to the actual words I said. They listened very closely to my words, but there was much more to it than that. I'm sure many judges made decisions in court based on the presence of fact, but I'm also positive that *the way* I said things helped me a great deal.

Let me do a simple demonstration here to illustrate how the way you say something can dramatically alter the meaning of what you've said.

Read this simple sentence:

I didn't say she stole the money.

Now, I want you to read each sentence below and simply emphasize the word in *bold italics* and notice how the meaning changes.

> *I* didn't say she stole the money.

> I *didn't* say she stole the money.

> I didn't *say* she stole the money.

> I didn't say *she* stole the money.

> I didn't say she *stole* the money.

> I didn't say she stole *the* money.

> I didn't say she stole the *money*.

See what I mean. It's pretty powerful what that simple shift in your intonation can achieve.

I didn't become a master communicator by taking a course or reading a book. What it took was thousands of hours of practice communicating. I learned firsthand that much of what passes for communication is really a very cheap imitation. Then, when I studied those seven leaders, I realized that they were (and are) really great communicators.

I realized that if I was going to become the successful Inspirational Leader that I wanted to be, I had to become a great communicator.

I knew that I already had that going for me.

I wish you could *hear* me say those words, because you'd feel the commitment and passion in every word.

In order to be a great communicator, you have to know what you're talking about. This comes from reading and studying and communicating, over and over again. In our industry, communication involves attending events and becoming an active, committed listener. Repeated listening makes you a better communicator, because the information you're communicating becomes more comfortable the more you hear it.

> *You become more confident as you become more competent.*

In court, we were always taught to be very concise. I remember my police sergeant saying, "Speak less. Say more." When I got involved in Network Marketing, I saw how perfectly this advice fit. If one of the secrets to success is getting people to know you, like you, and trust you, communication is absolutely the key: Being conscious of your tone of voice, the way you speak and the words you choose, being careful not to over-communicate.

Master the Art of Communication

Always be aware of the person you're talking to. When you're attempting to build a relationship with somebody during the recruiting process, ask open-ended questions.

People love this because we all love to talk about ourselves. Don't make the fatal flaw of interrupting them, unless it empowers them. During the process, if you ask somebody a question and then halfway through the answer you interrupt the person to talk more about yourself, you'll never get that person to like you. Instead, you'll offend that person, and he or she will never join your business.

Not interrupting people is paramount to becoming a successful communicator.

Okay, now I'm going to tell you the one and only time you're allowed to break that rule:

When you simply cannot help yourself.

It's called "Inspired interruption," and it's comes straight from the heart. Let me explain.

You and I are speaking and it's in the relationship-building phase of the prospecting process where I'm focused on getting to know you, like you and trust you (and having you do the same with me). You're in the midst of telling me about how you met your husband. The more you tell me, the more curious I'm becoming. Your story is such an unusual series of coincidences and I can't imagine what that was like for you. Nothing like that has ever happened to me. And right in the middle of your sentence... I interrupt you, saying something like:

"Natalie, that's incredible! I can't believe it. What did you think? What did you do? Tell me more..."

How do you think Natalie feels right then and there? Is she offended or is she pleased?

What I'm communicating by my Inspired Interruption is that I'm fascinated. I'm focused on Natalie. Really listening. I'm on the edge of my seat excited to learn more about her.

I passionately follow a powerful principle I learned from the Inspirational Leaders I studied in dealing with others, especially for communicating:

Validate Never Violate.

When you do not interrupt people you validate them. You honor them. And they appreciate you. That simple effort

136

builds know, like and trust naturally and automatically. On those occasions where you cannot help yourself because you're so excited and eager to know more, Inspired Interruption does the same thing.

Now, if you are someone with a foreign accent, you'll have to go the extra mile to make sure you are clearly understood. Many people have such strong accents that they're hard to understand. If you want to be successful in any business endeavor, you have to be understood. If your accent is so strong that it's hard for people to understand you, there are specific coaches that can assist you to develop a clearer use of the language and clean up your accent when you're speaking to other people.

Actors are an example of those who work at eliminating any trace of a foreign accent, depending on the role they are playing. Actors work with voice coaches and communication coaches all the time. Why not Network Marketers? You can find a local voice coach or a speaking coach online, and you'll discover that many of them are very reasonably priced.

Sidney Poitier is one actor who was determined to become a success, and working on his accent was a core part of his strategy. His is a rags-to-riches story.

He was raised in the Bahamas, the son of a tomato farmer. When he was 16 years old, he set out for New York City where he took a series of jobs, including dishwasher, longshoreman, butcher's assistant, porter, construction worker, salad washer, drugstore clerk, and soldier.

In 1945 he decided to take a stab at acting. He joined the American Negro Theatre, where he learned to eliminate his West Indian accent. Intent on transforming himself, Poitier practiced constantly, mimicking the voices he heard on the radio. If you've ever seen Sidney Poitier in film or on stage, I'm sure you'll agree that his rich, resonant voice is one of the most memorable things about him.

Singers with foreign accents often lose any trace of their accent while singing in other languages. A good example of this is the group Abba.

During the first few years of their remarkable career, none of them spoke enough English to place an order at McDonald's. But when you hear them sing, they are much easier to understand than many native English speakers.

It's crucial for actors and singers to develop their voices this way because their livelihood depends on it. What makes them great is their willingness and ability to do this.

Network Marketers need to be just as conscious. Our livelihood also depends on our ability to communicate with excellence.

Our business is about prospecting. It's about approaching new people, and often we have to do that on the telephone.

Frequently you'll have to leave a voicemail message. If you talk fast or slur your speech or use some dialect that's hard to understand on the phone, you'll limit your ability to get a call back. In order to get somebody to call you back, speak slowly and clearly. Speak concisely, leaving a short message that's to the point and easy to understand. That will affect the amount of people that call you back.

Become a Professional Storyteller

Network Marketers are professional storytellers. We contact people every day, and we're continually building relationships. One of the oldest sayings in this industry is, "Facts tell, stories sell." If you're trying to win somebody's heart, it's based on your ability to tell a story. If you take a look at all the millionaires in Network Marketing, you'll find that they're all professional storytellers. They tell the story of their company's products, of their opportunities, and of the experiences they've been through in the business.

More crucial than the details of any story is the *way* it's communicated. The words you use are important, but how you use them is even more important.

When I tell a story, it's the tone of my voice that creates the excitement people feel when they're listening to me. It's the energy and passion they feel when I talk about my products and my services that get their attention. This is extremely important.

You can talk to any leader in the industry; they'll all tell you the same thing.

The top income earners are the best storytellers.

There are two parts to becoming a great storyteller.

The first is the information you're seeking to share. Anybody can get all the information they need today just by going on the Internet.

The second part is the way you communicate: How you tell that story; the tones you use, the respect you pay to whoever is listening to you.

Be aware of the time. Be aware of your accent and tone. Be aware of how fast or slow you're talking. If you want somebody to really understand what you're saying, repeat one sentence, or a part of a sentence, with the best intonation. How you communicate your story is actually more important than the specific information points you're making.

Some Tips for Communicating with Prospects

Practice....

If you want to become good at anything you have to practice. To become a professional Network Marketer, you will need to develop the ability to tell a story and communicate better. I think that Malcom Gladwell's 10,000 hours theory applies here also. Get started right away. Join Toastmasters, listen to lots of audio leadership CDs and books.

Using Teaser Lines

Teaser lines are small, individual lines about our industry that are used to solicit interest from people in casual conversations.

There are all kinds of casual interactions with people where you can end up inviting somebody to look at your business. But when you first meet somebody in a social setting, **don't** invite that person to look at your business right away. Get to know them first.

As part of my own inviting and prospecting process, I often start conversations with people and just connect with them, learn about who and how they are. Whenever and wherever you can, simply open up and talk to people.

Here are some examples of teaser lines I've used:

> *Do you know anyone that would be interested in losing a bit of weight?*

> *Do you know anyone that would be interested in saving some money on those crazy cell phone bills?*

Do you know anyone that would be interested in saving some money at the gas pumps?

Power Lines

Power lines are one-paragraph, 30-second "commercials" that you use to instantly create interest in evaluating your opportunity, and at the same time, invite somebody to take a look at your business. As you create your own power lines, make sure they include the following elements:

1. **Introduce yourself and what you're doing.**

2. **Mention the industry and the trend you're involved in.**

3. **Validate the trend with a little bit of statistical information, media exposure or social proof.**

4. **Highlight a benefit or two that they can achieve if they were to do the same thing as you.**

5. **Ask a question and make sure you get a "yes" answer to it. By doing that, you can remove all of the fears or objections they might have.**

Here are two examples:

Hi my name is Ken Dunn. I'm working with a company that is focused helping people to change some simple eating habits and lose some weight. Our company is part of the wellness industry and is tackling a pandemic, Obesity. It's crazy; studies are showing that 60% of disposable income is controlled by people over the age of 50. Those baby boomers represent 60% of the population and they're all spending more than ever on products designed to get their lives back. Our company has designed an amazing product that you take as a meal replacement instead of your breakfast and you lose weight. I mean, do you know anyone that needs to lose a few pounds?

Hi my name is Ken Dunn. I'm working with a company that's bringing a product to market that helps to lower gas costs by increasing engine efficiencies. We are in a massive growth industry that helps average people fight back against crazy gas prices. We see it all over the news and we feel it ourselves at the pumps and it's not getting any better. Our product optimizes functionality and cleanliness of the engine with a liquid gas additive. It's just pennies per tank. Our research has proved that a cleaner engine runs better and conserves fuel. The net result is more miles to the gallon. Do you know anyone that would be interested in saving money at the pumps?

Communicate Your Way to Success

Developing your communication skills will increase your bank account, so do whatever is required for you to become an effective communicator.

Learn to tell great stories.

As your Network Marketing organization grows, you'll be required to speak effectively in public. You'll have lots of opportunities to address groups of people. You'll conduct trainings and coach new business partners. From prospecting to training, communication skills are essential. Good communication skills will increase your competence and confidence as well as your income!

Inspired Actions

Tips to Improve Your Communication

1. Be detail-oriented in every aspect of your speech; don't over-communicate.

2. Speak less and say more.

3. Never interrupt unless empowering, Validate never Violate.

4. If you have a strong accent, speak slower.

5. Be sure you know a lot about the subject you're speaking about.

6. It's okay not to know something or understand a certain point— a strong communicator admits a lack of knowledge right up front and that leads to trust.

7. Learn better speaking skills by listening to thousands of hours of Audio CDs and books.

8

Build Confidence

*"Happiness and self-confidence come naturally when you feel
you are moving and progressing toward becoming the very best person you can
possibly be."*

BRIAN TRACY

Confidence is a quality that is often misunderstood in our business.

A few years ago, I was having dinner with a teammate of mine
from Florida. During the course of our conversation, he told
me that he wasn't happy with his level of success and that he
didn't have any credibility. That really struck me because this
guy was a really successful entrepreneur. He had tons of
credibility in my opinion. He just hadn't been successful in
Network Marketing yet.

I realized that what he really meant was that he lacked
confidence. He wasn't confident in what he was doing.

**Often in our industry, people confuse
credibility and confidence, and this can be
a dream killer.**

As my teammate shared his perceived lack of credibility,
suddenly a story from my childhood popped into my head,
and I shared it with him.

I was in the second grade, just a young whippersnapper, and one day I was being bullied by a fellow my age. This young fellow thought he was a tough guy and we started pushing each other around. He spat in my face. I was so enraged by this that it just drove me right off the deep end.

I grabbed him, but he managed to get away from me. He knew how angry I was and he was afraid. He started running, and I ran after him as hard as I could. We ran for several minutes through the school, through the playground. I just wanted to rip him apart when I caught him.

He ran around a corner, and as I came around the corner, there he stood— suddenly completely confident with six of his best friends flanking him, three on each side. They were all staring at me. I stopped dead in my tracks. I became instantly afraid. I didn't know what to do.

All seven of these guys now came at me and I ran without stopping for three miles, all the way back to my house.

This experience came into my head as I sat there looking at this incredibly successful entrepreneur who was saying he had no credibility. No confidence. So I told him that story. I said,

"Listen, as I ran around that corner and saw those guys standing there, I didn't only see that one fellow who had just spat in my face. I saw these seven guys, and I was instantly full of fear where I'd been angry before."

I likened that experience to how he should deal with his perceived lack of credibility. You see, the weakest of the bunch was that little guy who had just spat in my face. But now, flanked by his friends, I couldn't even see the little guy— all I saw the total of seven boys.

In order to get over your own lack of credibility, use this simple idea based on that story.

Make a list of all the great things you have done in your life, and then add to it all the greatest attributes of your personality.

Write this list in a single column on the left side of a clean piece of paper. Now, in a second column to the right of that, write down "lack of success in Network Marketing."

What you have to realize is that when people are evaluating you and your Network Marketing company, they don't see your lack of success. They see all the other stuff. The lack of success is just a made up idea that is stuck in your head. It isn't real.

Once I shared this story with my teammate, he got it right away. He created a list of all of his good personality traits and accomplishments in life. At the top of the list he wrote, *"I have credibility in life."*

To this day, he carries that list around with him everywhere, and he reads it several times per day. In fact, he reads it so much that he has forgotten all about the fact that he had not been as successful as he wanted to be. Of course, his prospecting and closing success has gone up 100%.

People are not going to see the little guy in the middle. They'll see the group of seven standing before them. Create your own list, and your confidence will go through the roof.

I told my teammate, "Here's the bottom line. You already have everything you require to be successful in this business." I shared with this entrepreneur several things about his own life that were successful. I pointed out several positive qualities about this incredible man. He was a millionaire. He was charismatic. He was an amazing business man. As I was explaining to him how much I respected and appreciated him, I saw his back straighten up and a huge smile appear on his face.

I asked him, "How do you feel right now, at this very moment?"

He said, "I feel great. I know these things are true."

I told him,

"That's *all* other people see."

Act in Spite of Fear

Even though I've made this sound very simple (and it really is that simple), there will be times when the telephone sitting in front of you suddenly seems to weigh 100 pounds. I'll let you in on a little secret— even though I had been confident in my other endeavors, I was not at all confident when I began my Network Marketing career.

I was very nervous about calling the first people I called in this business… *but I called them anyway.*

Act in spite of your fear.

We all go through this. You have to be able to pick up the phone if you want to get the results. Tell yourself that you're just looking for people that are looking. You may have to go through a lot of people. Most people do.

Write this down in big, bold letters:

Eight out of 10 people will say "No."

If you understand this, then you'll realize that you just need to get through those eight out of the 10 people, over and over again.

The key to this business is not how much you actually *know*, but how *excited* you are. Success in Network Marketing is 99% attitude and one percent aptitude. It doesn't matter if you know anything about your opportunity. All you need to know is that it's the most incredible opportunity in the world.

We'd all rather have ignorance on fire than knowledge on ice. Let your excitement fuel your actions and you'll discover that because you are so excited, you will act with confidence.

Be Passionate!

Be passionate! Passion is fueled by belief. Stay connected to the successful people in your upline so they can assist you to fuel your belief. If you do this, your passion will go up, your belief level will go up, and this will be transmitted through the words you say— to others and yourself.

If you're not somebody that is normally pumped up, do whatever you have to do to get yourself pumped up. And then jump into it:

> *"Sue, I'm really excited! I've found a great opportunity that I think will assist me to get where I want to go financially in life, and I want you to hear about it*

because I think there's something here for you also. When can we get together?"

(This is for somebody in your warm market.) Ask them directly— all you want to do is put them in front of the information.

It's Not About the Money

When I think about the seven Inspirational Leaders that have so impacted my journey, I realize that every one of them was supremely confident in what they were doing— even though every one of them had flaws of one kind or another. You never saw those flaws, though. You looked at them, and you just saw incredible confidence.

You might be looking at yourself and saying, "I have no credibility because I haven't made money." But here's the thing: credibility doesn't come from the money.

I know many people that have gotten into this business that have never made a cent, but they have this natural inherent ability to recruit other people, to connect with other people. Their confident qualities, their successes in life, all their best qualities are shining through.

Every time I introduce somebody to my business or I get a chance to coach somebody, I have them point out all their best qualities— to me and to themselves.

This enables them to recruit with those qualities in front of them, with those thoughts in their mind, and they stop worrying about the credibility they perceive isn't there because they haven't made any money yet. They're just limiting themselves with that mindset. And, it's not real. They just made that up.

Don't Let Your Limitations Limit You

Let's face it— everybody has limitations. When I get a chance to coach someone, I explore with that person the incredible confidence those seven inspirational leaders had. Even though each of them had limitations in their lives, they didn't let those limitations shine through. Limitations are not the light. Limitations only exist in darkness.

Are you familiar with this quote from Marianne Williamson's book *A Return to Love?*

> *Our deepest fear is not that we are inadequate. Our deepest fear is that we are powerful beyond measure. It is our light, not our darkness, that most frightens us. We ask ourselves, who am I to be brilliant, gorgeous, talented and fabulous? Actually, who are you <u>not</u> to be? You are a child of God. Your playing small doesn't serve the world. There's nothing enlightened about shrinking so that other people won't feel insecure around you. We were born to make manifest the glory of God that is within us. It's not just in some of us; it's in everyone. And as we let our own light shine, we unconsciously give other people permission to do the same. As we are liberated from our own fear, our presence automatically liberates others.*

Pierre Trudeau is an example of someone who had unwavering confidence and charisma in the face of strong opponents. Many Canadians, myself included, highly regard him, but he inspired fierce antipathy among those who disagreed with his political decisions and policies. One historian, Michael Bliss, put it this way:

"Trudeau is one of the most admired and most disliked of all Canadian prime ministers."

Trudeau's confidence had everything to do with him becoming one of the most transformative figures in Canada's history.

Gandhi is another person who recognized the value of confidence. He said,

"The history of the world is full of men who rose to leadership, by sheer force of self-confidence, bravery, and tenacity."

How's that for some inspired coaching? Gandhi's saying you can become a leader, not by being particularly gifted or by the absence of any limitations, but by the sheer force of your own confidence.

Steve Jobs and John F. Kennedy both had severe health issues, but neither of them allowed these limitations to lessen their confidence or their impact in the world.

Kennedy had chronic pain and digestive problems his entire adult life. Steve Jobs had a rare form of pancreatic cancer back in 2003 and recently was in the news again when people began questioning his health. They wondered if his cancer had returned or if he'd had a heart attack. Through it all, he confidently continued to do what he does best— lead Apple.

Just like these leaders, the reason why some individuals become so incredibly successful in Network Marketing and others don't is that, while we all have limitations, while we all lack some type of credibility, those who make it to the top don't let those limitations hold them back.

Inspirational Leaders focus on the things they're really great at and build upon those characteristics.

A vital key to being successful in Network Marketing is knowing what your strengths are, really focusing on those strengths, and letting those good qualities come through in all your dealings with people.

For instance, when you focus on improving your communication skills, defining your why, being detail-oriented, and increasing your gravitational pull, you'll build up other areas of your credibility, even if you're not making money yet.

No matter what our vocation is, we're all learning to master it each and every day. The difference between those who create phenomenal results and those who don't is that those of us who do have learned to master creating results based on the skills and strengths we already bring to the table while we're developing those other areas that require a bit more attention.

And that's exactly what you can do too!

Inspired Actions

Keys for Building Confidence

- Know your existing strengths and skills.

- Develop and improve any areas that require improvement, always letting your existing qualities shine through.

- Make a list of your greatest personality strengths and your greatest successes in life and carry it around with you.

- Focus on your strengths, not your limitations.

9

Pay Attention to the Details

"A man's accomplishments in life are the
cumulative effect of his attention to detail."

JOHN FOSTER DULLES

In this chapter, I'll cover how to develop the ability to be organized and focus on the details of creating a successful business.

Maybe you've just joined a company, or perhaps you've been in the industry for a while and you're looking for a refresher. Either way, the key to success in this business is getting started properly, and this chapter will spell things out for you.

All of the inspirational leaders I studied were meticulous about how they lived their lives and their callings.

For example, Mother Teresa had a sharp analytical mind and a keen eye for detail. Extremely conscientious, she was efficient and thorough in her work and took pride in a job well done. Mother was adept at using her hands to create or fix things, and exacting attention to detail and careful craftsmanship were her forte.

Mother Teresa liked to organize, categorize, and arrange everything into a logical system— she was very uncomfortable with disorganization.

Besides being a stickler for details, she had a strong desire to continually improve, refine, and perfect *everything*. Mother Teresa was especially particular about her diet, hygiene, and health habits. Her tastes were simple and understated, yet highly refined.

You'll want to develop a similar attention to details as you set up your business in ways that will allow it to soar.

The Essentials

This business is simple and there are only a few essentials required to truly be successful. Being organized is right up at the top, and equally important is having an effective and efficient system— and *using* it.

Connecting with people is key, and there are a multitude of details that you'll want to pay attention to if you desire to reach the top of your game.

The more detail-oriented you are about the essentials, the less you'll miss opportunities and the faster you'll drive your business forward.

I will provide you with strategies for creating a master list of people to contact, and I'll show you how you can continually add to it, many times for free by utilizing the power of the Internet. But in order to really master this business, you must learn to focus on key details and organize your time each day.

When I began my business, I had no idea how to actually get started properly. I had passion, and yes as I've said, ignorance on fire is better than knowledge on ice any day. But if you know the basics, then you can go crazy and build an incredible business— it all starts with the fundamentals. Every time you personally bring somebody new into this industry, you get something out of what that person saw in the opportunity and what they saw in you.

Let's Get Organized

The key to your success is being organized from the day you get started.

You're starting a business!

That's it, plain and simple.

You must have some space set up for yourself that you can operate from. Understand from day one that you are starting an international enterprise, and in order to do that successfully, you have to set it up properly. *Get organized.*

Once you've designated the space in your house, set up your home office. If you've already got one, check that it's set up properly. The tools of your trade are very simple: A phone, paper and a pen. Make sure you have these things available and ready for your daily work.

The Home Office

It's vitally important that you designate space in your house that you can call your home office. It doesn't have to be a separate room. It can literally be a space in your kitchen. My first home office was a corner in my bedroom. I kept my notes, my pen, my paper, and some price lists for my products on my dresser.

I called this my office because that's all I had available at the time for my business, but I took it very seriously, and I treated it with respect. Nothing else got in the way— it was a priority.

Eventually I graduated from that space on my dresser to a closet. To this day, my set up is pretty much the same. I have a desk with a computer, a little calculator, some price lists and brochures from my company, a list of my contacts and prospects, my follow-up charts, and my agenda.

That's all there is and... It's all right there.

If you set yourself up from the start to be ready for success, your chances of achieving that success will be far greater.

Once you've set up your home office, *get out of the house*. The beautiful thing about this business is that you can do it any way you want. When you start to venture outside of your home to build your business, it's crucial that you are already set up properly for success that way, too.

You Are a Master Franchiser

The list of names that you write when you first get started is the foundation of your business. At the same time you write your list, you also have to understand your business.

Regardless of what company you're in, ask yourself, "What is my goal in this company, in this business?"

Here's my answer:

I'm building an international distribution process.

The way I see it, you're creating a way of moving products from point A to point B; from the manufacturer right to the end consumer. Your goal is to create a network of thousands of people that buy your company's products and either resell them or consume them themselves. This is your key to financial freedom.

Picture yourself as a *master franchiser*— as someone who is opening a new franchise in your state, in your city. Your goal is to get people to buy franchises. (Think McDonald's, Subway, Supercuts.) The way you make money as a master franchiser is to go out and present your opportunity and your products to people. Your goal at the end of the day is to find people who are willing to invest and open franchises of their own. In this case, it's a micro-franchise, but nonetheless, it's definitely a franchise-like system.

Create Passion

Now that you've set up your office, created your list, and you understand your system, you're ready to generate some passion.

Become familiar with your products and services. I know many people consider this a cliché. It may be over-used, but unless it's fully understood, you cannot succeed in this business:

> **Understand your products intimately and use them passionately— become a product of your products.**

If you don't have a personal story to share about your product or service, how do you expect somebody else to get passionate about it and want to follow you in your business?

The biggest thing I can tell you is to become a student. Become a student of your business. Leaders are readers, and readers are leaders. Pick up a great book, and learn all you can about the Network Marketing industry. It's a massive industry, and we all should to become experts on it.

Some excellent books are:

- *The New Professionals: The Rise of Network Marketing*
- *Your First Year in Network Marketing*
- *The Greatest Networker in the World*
- *Good to Great*
- And *How to Win Friends and Influence People.*

You can find these books on Amazon, Barnes and Noble or at your local library. Start reading one of them today. Become a passionate reader and leader.

Logs, Journals, and Agendas Will Save Your Life

Anyone who knows me will be the first to tell you that I have developed a keen ability to handle many different tasks simultaneously, to multitask. Have you ever known a true multi-tasker and wondered how they ever manage to keep it all straight?

My Secret

I keep track of all my appointments and contacts in my Smart Phone. I also carry a simple white steno pad with me everywhere I go.

At the start of every day, I take ten minutes to get organized. I open the steno pad to a clean page. On the top section of the spiral metal spine, I write the names and numbers of everyone that I have to call that day, along with a brief explanation of the details.

On the bottom of the page, I write a list of the tasks that I plan to accomplish that day. As I go through the day, I check off the things that I accomplish and add anything that comes up to the existing lists. The next day I start over by compiling new lists and carrying forward anything pertinent from the day before.

Here's another other important point. Every great leader I can think of has one thing in common.

They take 10 or 15 minutes every morning to collect themselves and set themselves up for the day.

When I realized this and adapted it myself, my life became clear and focused. In those 10 minutes, they review the day before, prioritize their outstanding tasks, and read a few pages from a good book.

As you become more successful, you'll become busier. It comes with the territory. If you wait until you are successful to get organized, you will never become successful. Start today by developing your own system of time management.

I strongly suggest that you start with Franklin Covey's system. Over a billion dollars per year (the company's sales revenue) must mean something! Regardless of what system you use, use something. We're simply not designed to hold everything in our heads.

If the greatest leaders in the world use agendas, logs, and journals, shouldn't you?

You can now breathe a sigh of relief to know that these leaders are not superhuman and you don't have to be either. They're just meticulous. They use time management tools and techniques to become detailed-oriented multi-taskers. You can, too!

Inspired Actions

How to Become More Detail-Oriented

1. Keep a list.

2. Prioritize each item on your list.

3. When you start a task, finish the task.

4. Take the first 10 minutes of every day to get organized and create your day's task list.

5. Use an agenda or PDA.

6. Spend 20 minutes every day reading a good book.

7. When you are with someone, make it a point to notice personal details.

8. Keep a follow-up journal related to your business.

10

Create a Gravitational Pull

"Conscious of the power of connection, the best leaders take responsibility for relating with others on a regular basis."

JOHN C. MAXWELL

In this chapter, I'll share some techniques that I use to create *gravitational pull,* and I'll show you how to attract people by creating your own.

Understanding gravitational pull has had the biggest impact on turning my life around. I realized that the inspirational leaders I studied had this ability to attract others, and I knew if I wanted to get better, I required it. This is the one area of change that I have focused the most attention on, and it has had the biggest impact on my success. The great part is that you can learn gravitational pull. It's not a skill or ability that is reserved for the world's elite.

I've put together some simple techniques that, if you practice them, will make your gravitational pull go through the roof. More people will like you than ever before. If more people like you, then they'll start to trust you more, and your prospecting ability will hit the stratosphere— and when it does, your ability to prospect will become second nature and hugely successful.

What Is Gravitational Pull?

Gravitational pull is the ability to capture the attention of another person. It's the natural (or practiced, as in my case) ability to grab another person's interest.

Gravitational pull is that almost magical attraction some people seem to have when they walk in a room. All eyes turn to them.

Even walking through a crowd, not saying a word, people just seem to gravitate towards people like this. Most top leaders in the world have this type of force field around them that spontaneously draws people towards them.

Every one of the seven leaders I studied had this magnetic quality. It wasn't forced. Instead, it was amazingly natural. Mother Teresa, just quietly walking down a street, would have thousands of people flocking to her, even before she was a household name around the world. She was quiet and unassuming, but her gravitational pull was incredibly strong and attractive.

John F. Kennedy also had a strong gravitational pull. He was the epitome of charisma. He knew how to project himself into the hearts of the American people. Gandhi possessed this quality as well. All of the inspirational leaders I studied were recognized as leaders in large part because of their tremendous ability to influence others and their appealing magnetism.

They were fascinating individuals who continue to be intriguing to the rest of us. I'm still learning about them—there's always more to learn about the secrets of success and personal strength they possess.

As I seriously focused on becoming a better person, I noticed something happening— it seemed that I always had people that wanted to be around me. Suddenly I never lacked for somebody to go to dinner with.

A Book that Changed My Life

A few years ago I traveled to Asia for five weeks, where I visited five different countries on business. Hong Kong is the longest leg of the flight, and I always fly first class, because on the plane they have these incredible new pod seats that are almost like little rooms. The seat rolls out flat into a bed, a canopy comes over the top, and you can effectively shut out the world.

On this particular trip, just before I boarded the plane, I went into a store at the airport to buy a bottle of water, and at the cash register the title of a book just jumped out of me: *How to Make People Like You in 90 Seconds or Less*.

I bought the book, threw it in my bag, and headed for the plane. Anything you can do to get people to like you better is important, because people only join the business for three reasons. This book promised to have me learn more about one of them.

The plane took off, and I discovered that my reclining seat didn't work. So there I was, beginning a 15-hour flight to Hong Kong. The plane was booked solid and I'm stuck in a broken seat. There wasn't another empty seat on the plane. To make matters worse, my individual personal entertainment center didn't work either— no movies, no music.

With nothing else to do, I started flipping through *How to Make People Like You in 90 Seconds or Less*, and instantly I was blown away by how this book spoke to me. It was the essence of everything that I'd ever learned about gravitational pull.

The author, Nicholas Boothman, reveals the secret of how you get people to like you in a minute and a-half or less. I read this book *four times* on the way to Hong Kong. In approximately 185 pages, it covered all the essentials of building rapport with people and learning how to connect with them.

Over the next three weeks as I traveled around Asia, I was on 14 different airplanes, and on each flight I just kept reading this book over and over again. When I got back to my office, I put the book on my assistant's desk and told her, "Wendy, you need to find this author. I don't care if he lives in Milan or New York City, I want to go and meet him. Get me an appointment with him." I wanted to meet this guy!

A few hours later, my assistant came back to me, giggling and saying, "Well, you won't need a plane ticket. Nicholas Boothman lives 20 minutes down the road from your house!"

The irony is that Boothman spent 25 years in international photojournalism. He was a top advertising photographer in the fashion industry, traveling to Milan and Rome and Portugal and New York City. So for him to be living down the road from me in Canada was just unbelievable.

Since Nick lives nearby, we've had the opportunity to spend time together, and we've become friends. The concepts that he teaches on how to get people to like you and the pitfalls he shares about how to avoid them not liking you are directly in line with everything I've learned about not offending people. Remember, "Validate Never Violate."

How I Created Gravitational Pull

At the end of that first year when my leaders confronted me and told me what an evil person I had become, I was, at first, really confused. Up until then, I always had received pretty decent feedback about being able to make great first impressions. However, I came to the realization that my problem wasn't so much the first impression... It was my lasting impression, how I dealt with people over the long-term.

In my own life, I had the ability to get people to like me quickly, but I was terrible at keeping that positive connection. A friend pointed out to me that I had the uncanny ability to create a friendship with somebody and then ruin that friendship within the first 15 minutes.

I guess I never really thought a lot about people. I had to come to the realization that I didn't really care very much about others.

By studying the seven leaders and observing how charismatic they were and how skilled they were at building relationships, I finally realized what an important quality this was.

I knew that if I was going to be the leader that I wanted to be— an inspirational leader, a truly great leader— I had to create this same all-encompassing gravitational pull in myself.

Over time I have learned to treat people the way I am able to treat them in those first couple of minutes after meeting them. I've learned to stay consistent with the way I treated people in those first 90 seconds.

I understood the basics of this, but I had not yet developed the focus or the ability to build and sustain lasting relationships. This was a really tough challenge for me.

Keys to Connecting with Others

First, make eye contact with as many people as you can. The first time you make eye contact with someone, smile! (From earlier reading you know why).

In the beginning, this was really hard for me to do. Remember, I had a policeman's personality. Whenever I looked at somebody before, I would automatically think the worst of them. It was part of my job; simply ingrained in me. But now I play a little mindset game with myself.

Whenever I see somebody new, in my mind I say, "That's a great person; I want to be their friend." When I say that, my heart lightens up, my eyes soften, and I spontaneously smile at them.

I don't smile at them as if I'm a two-bit car salesperson trying to sell them a used clunker; I just flash them a gentle smile, showing a bit of teeth, and I look them right in the eye. I'm really saying, "Hi, how are you doing?" with my eyes and my smile. And any time I have the opportunity, I always introduce myself and extend my hand in a handshake as soon as possible.

Whenever I shake someone's hand, I'm always very cautious about that handshake, because it's such an important part of creating gravitational pull.

When some people shake your hand, they nearly squeeze the blood right out you. You feel like they're going to rip your hand right off. Then there's the other extreme: People with what I call a "wet noodle" handshake. What you want to achieve is a perfect interaction with somebody else through the combination of your eyes, smile, introduction, and handshake. That first handshake is very important overall for the beginnings of a long-term relationship.

People with gravitational pull are very charismatic. When they meet someone, you'll observe them looking directly into that person's eyes. You see their sincere smile. You see that open-handed handshake, that perfect grip. Whenever they are with you, they are really _with_ you.

This was something I had to learn to develop.

In the past, whenever I was talking to somebody, my mind was clearly elsewhere. This is something that my friends pointed out to me as one of my biggest flaws. I came to see how counterproductive this was.

I mean, there I was, trying to build a relationship with somebody, but because my mind was somewhere else, they would automatically conclude that I didn't really want to be around them. When I thought about this, I realized that I would have interpreted my behavior exactly the same way.

Now, I live by the adage that when I'm with somebody, I'm really _with them._

It doesn't matter what else is going on in my life. When I'm communicating with somebody, I block everything else out. The top leaders in the world all have this ability to block out the rest of the world when they're talking with someone. It may be natural or they may have developed it, and they all possess it.

You've heard me say that a millionaire in Network Marketing is somebody that has a million friends. That was and is a profound statement for me, because I had to face the fact that I never really cared about being with anyone before.

As I told you, Michael Clouse taught me that people are only going to join the business if they know you, like you, and trust you.

What can you take away from these two keys?

Well, if you want to make a million dollars in Network Marketing, you have to make more friends. The only way you can make more friends is if people like you. If they like you and they're your friends, they're more likely to join your business. And the easiest way in the world to create friends is to actively be interested in other people.

Part of my own personal development process was realizing that I truly *did* like people, and I really *did* want them to like me.

All good leaders I know take a keen and active interest in the people around them. Whenever I get to know someone now, I ask open-ended questions about their life— NOT simply as a tool to engage them in conversation, but because I sincerely want to know. I ask questions about their family, their occupation, what they like to do for recreation, hobbies, likes and loves. What I'm looking for most is the one thing that's more important to them than anything else. I really want to get to know them. I want to have that kind of relationship with everybody I meet.

Imagine what your life will be like when you achieve a goal like that?

Your goal should be to make a million friends!

The fastest way to do that is to get people to talk, get them to open up. The more I did this, the more I discovered that people love to talk about themselves. As I developed a strong gravitational pull, I learned to speak less and say more. I became skilled at asking questions and letting others talk.

169

I learned that it's very important to avoid interrupting anybody (and please remember my exception to the rule about "Inspired Interruptions."). In the past, I had this incredibly bad habit: Whenever I'd ask somebody a question, right in the midst of their answer I would inevitably interrupt them. Right in the middle of their comment, I'd jump in to get *my* point across.

I didn't see this as a bad habit— I just thought I had a lot of value to add, and I couldn't wait for them to finish, so I could tell them all about my great idea. I was very impatient with people. I offended people, and I never knew why.

It's so easy to offend people if you interrupt them. True leaders are always cognizant of other people's feelings.

If you are the type of person that interrupts others during conversation, you're just hurting yourself. It's harder to get people to like you, and you'll have a hard time getting a positive response from people about your business if you have this habit.

Perhaps you're saying, "Oh, my gosh— that's me!" That's what happened to me. I realized that this was one of the biggest problems I had. It was one of the reasons so many people disliked me. I realized that none of leaders I studied were like this.

Details, Details

There are many small pieces to learn to create stronger relationships more quickly. How you look is important. What you wear is important. In my case, I decided to hire a professional shopper to assist me with creating a wardrobe that worked.

How you smell is also important. Have you ever met somebody who has halitosis? Some people have this issue and don't realize it. The smallest details of how you come across to somebody else will affect your ability to build a relationship.

Be cognizant of other people's space. Respect the three-foot rule. I've known some people who would get two inches from my face and start talking. People like this have no idea how offensive this is to 97% of the population.

I've had the opportunity to travel to 25 different countries around the world, and I've realized that the customs in each country are very diverse. The way we interact with each other in North America can be quite offensive to somebody in India or Indonesia. When you're traveling overseas, learn to be aware of the customs of each country you visit and interact with people accordingly.

If you are traveling abroad, go to the Web site of that country and look up "customs and protocols." You'll find everything you need to know about what to do— and, more importantly, what NOT to do— to create better gravitational pull.

Every piece of the puzzle, no matter how small, matters.

When I started learning about gravitational pull, I applied all of these things to my life. Now, when I interact with somebody, I'm fully with them, no matter what else is going on in my life. As I told you, I always start with a open smile and an open handshake. I tell them who I am, and I ask open-ended questions. I've learned to be patient with people, and I've discovered that I truly enjoy and care about them.

Creating Your Own Gravitational Pull

If you want to be successful in life focus on creating your own gravitational pull. Once you know what gravitational pull is, you can learn to create it, and then you can learn to maintain it and make it an integral part of who you are.

In many ways, creating gravitational pull starts with your appearance. Strive to look your best. This is not about vanity or appearances for appearance sake. Looking good feels good, and when you feel good, others are drawn to you. (Remember that research about your smile.)

You may say, "Well, people just have to accept me the way I am." There's no problem with this as long as you can accept who you are. If you're happy with the success you've had in life, if you're happy with what you're getting out of life right now, that's great, but...

In my world there's nothing wrong with trying to become a better person and creating gravitational pull.

Frankly, I think everybody should make sure they appear at their best all the time. If you want to create great gravitational pull, as shallow as this may sound, people are attracted to people that feel good and look good. It's not about how much you weigh or whether you were blessed with magazine model good looks. It's an overall positive feeling someone receives from their first contact with you.

If you're really serious about increasing your gravitational pull, do what I did. Take a serious interest in looking the best you can, both with your own physical appearance and how you dress. Those that are taking leadership seriously and trying to create that pull try their best to look their best. In order to do this, you must first respect and value yourself, and this becomes the foundation that allows you to extend that to other people.

172

Always dress with the styles of the day. You don't have to drop thousands of dollars on clothes, but if your wardrobe is full of bright green paisley shirts that's not going to help you to increase gravitational pull, unless you're at a 1970's high school reunion! How you look is important.

Next, how you approach someone is important. Make eye contact, have a firm (not crushing, not limp) handshake. Be aware of your tone of voice.

It's very important to slow down a little when you speak. Make your voice welcoming and inviting. Be precise with your words. These are all areas for continual improvement. All the leaders I studied made this kind of personal development an ongoing priority.

Nick Boothman's book, *How to Make People Like You in 90 Seconds or Less*, is the bible of gravitational pull. I first coined the term "gravitational pull" years before I read this book, but Nick put it all into perspective for me.

In fact, if I'd have read Nick Boothman's book first, I might not have ever developed the term gravitational pull. It's appearance. It's eye contact. It's how you shake somebody's hand. If you're in a foreign country it's understanding the customs of that country so you don't offend someone.

Gravitational pull is about honestly wanting to get to know somebody. When you're with someone, really be with that person. Ask people open-ended questions, and then let them respond. It all works together.

If you create a really strong gravitational pull, people will like you more. If they like you more, they'll be more inclined to join your business.

Dealing with Your New Gravitational Pull

As you begin to develop a great gravitational pull, suddenly many people will want to be around you and hang out with you and spend time with you and get to know you better— and you won't be used to this at all. You may begin to feel a little overwhelmed or put undue pressure and stress on yourself to perform in this situation. How do you deal with it?

My advice is to stay *real*. When your gravitational pull starts to increase, just be yourself and continue to be real.

Always have respect for yourself in the process. Retain sufficient time for yourself. When you have that type of gravitational pull, you're going to require time to unwind. I most often spend quiet time with my family, and I recognize that this is vitally important for me.

When you have lots of people around you all the time, it's vital that you fulfill your commitments— every single one of them. Make sure that you develop an attitude of gratitude. Your modus operandi should be to always under promise and over deliver. Don't say anything that you're not going to live up to. When you develop huge gravitational pull, you want to be very cognizant of how and what you say to other people, and be careful to say things that empower others.

What if you're a Type A personality like me who has a tendency to be constantly moving at *Mach II With Your Hair On Fire* (as Richard Brooke would say), how can you slow down, become more patient, and become more effective in your communications?

As a police officer, I had a tendency to be demanding, controlling, and impatient— in a lot of cases lives depended on me being this way. Those qualities were strongly ingrained in me. But how can you create a strong sense of gravitational pull if you are completely impatient?

It's all about developing the right mindset. You have to realize that your standards will be higher than those around you.

You must apply your standards to yourself, while at the same time letting everybody else be who they are.

Learn to let things go.

Understand that often other people will let you down, and you have to just let it roll off you like water off a duck's back. Accept people for who they are, and understand that their strengths may not be the same as yours.

Remember, Rome wasn't built in a day. I speak from experience; learning patience has been one of the biggest challenges I've ever had in my life. I want everything yesterday. I know that I can move at a million miles an hour, but most people around me can't or don't want to.

I've become so much more aware of the fact that we have to love and respect everybody for who they are. It's really important to stay even-keeled and patient— with yourself first and then with those around you. Bottom line: get to know your personality. Once you do then you will be able to play to your strengths.

Creating Gravitational Pull is really the essence of leadership. Many of the things that we have covered in this chapter are all great leadership qualities. Leadership starts with learning your own strengths & weaknesses and then deciding to play to the strengths and work on the flaws.

The greatest leaders are those that learn to lead one's self first!

There's tremendous power in developing your own unique gravitational pull.

With it comes the responsibility to use it wisely to serve others.

That's what we'll cover in the next chapter.

Inspired Actions

Simple Steps to Increasing Gravitational Pull

1. Read *How to Make People Like You in 90 Seconds or Less* by Nicholas Boothman.

2. Always try your best to look your best.

3. Work on truly listening to others.

4. Avoid others' personal space.

5. Ask open-ended relationship-building questions.

6. When you're with someone, really be _with_ them.

7. Be sincerely interested in other people.

8. Do not interrupt unless it's empowering.

9. Smile and introduce yourself all the time.

10. Create a goal to make two new friends every day.

11

Serve Others

"In this life we cannot do great things.
We can only do small things with great love.

MOTHER TERESA OF CALCUTTA

Robert Macauley is the founder of AmeriCares, a relief organization that distributes critical medicines and medical supplies to the world's poor in times of disaster. He's often been in the position of raising money for the organization himself, and he credits Mother Teresa with teaching him how to be a beggar. "I learned from the best!" he said in a *Guideposts* article (*Mother T & Me*, Guideposts, April 1, 2006).

He and Mother had visited several orphanages in Guatemala and were flying to Mexico. This is where his lesson on begging took place. When the flight attendant brought the food (this was back in the day when you actually got a meal on a flight), Mother Teresa spoke up. She asked the stewardess how much the meal would cost in U.S. dollars. "About a dollar," came the answer. Then Mother Teresa asked if she could she have a dollar for the poor if she gave her meal back.

The startled flight attendant went to consult with the pilot, returning a few minutes later with the news. "Yes, Mother," she said, "You may have the money for the poor."

Mother Teresa handed over her tray. Bob Macauley felt compelled to hand his over as well, as there was no way he could eat in front of her. Suddenly people across the aisle began handing in their trays too.

Finally the flight attendant said over the loud speaker:

For anyone who gave up their meal, the airlines would donate a dollar to the poor.

In the end, the entire 129 passengers gave up their meals, including the crew.

But Mother Teresa wasn't finished. She then asked if the airlines would give her all the meals. She knew that they couldn't be reused, and she wanted to give them to the poor. This request was graciously granted— but... then what?

How to transport these meals? Mother Teresa had one more request: Could the airlines allow her to use one of their trucks? Amazingly, this too was granted, and off she went to a poor section of Mexico City. Swarms of hungry children gathered around that truck, eager for the meals she began handing out.

On the way back to the airport, Mother Teresa explained to Bob Macauley, "It's easy to ask when you're doing it for the poor!"

We All Think of Philanthropy Someday...

When I really started to study the seven leaders that I profiled earlier in the book, it didn't surprise me at all that they were all incredible givers. Obviously, Gandhi and Mother Teresa gave their entire lives, but this may not be so obvious with business leaders. However, you probably know that Bill Gates is one of the biggest givers (philanthropists) in the world today.

Mr. Gates' charitable foundations have given tens of billions of dollars to a whole host of good causes.

Wouldn't you like to be a philanthropist? Haven't we all thought at one time or another about giving?

Unfortunately for most of us, as soon as the thought enters our minds, it is quickly replaced with negative thoughts of the bills that are adding up, the mortgage payments that are due, the educations that need to be paid for, and our philanthropic thoughts are put on hold.

The more I studied Inspirational Leaders, the more I realized that service to others was ingrained in their souls.

I wanted so desperately to become a better person that I started to really devote time to thinking about how I could serve others. While collecting my thoughts, I realized that service to others is not about how much money you can give to your favorite charity; it is much deeper and much simpler than that.

If you want to be a great Bill Gates-like philanthropist tomorrow, then you have to respect others more than yoveryu respect yourself today. You need to wake up every morning and begin every day by asking yourself, "Who can I make feel good about themselves today?" People do not become philanthropists automatically. They grow into it.

If you take a look back through Bill Gates' life, he has always been a caring, loving, giving person. There are clues through his entire life that he went out of his way to do things for others. Most times in the early days, it was random acts of kindness, politeness, and innocent acts, but it was all serving in nature.

Where Service to Others Really Begins

As I started to really understand where service to others actually starts, I became really excited.

I realized that by focusing on gravitational pull, I was simultaneously serving others. I was doing what great leaders do!

This was awesome for me because I was "killing two birds with one stone." Sorry for the poor analogy, but you get my point. I'm still aggressive and want as much as possible today, so if I can tackle two traits at the same time, I'm excited.

Here's the deal: In the last chapter, we talked about increasing your attraction to other people by getting them to like you, being sincerely interested in them, and making them feel good when you are around them.

Well, if you do these things, aren't you simultaneously serving them? You are making them feel good about themselves. Let's say that prior to your interaction with a person, he or she is having a bad day, and then you come up and greet them with a welcoming smile, a calm gesture, and then you follow up with an sincere interest in them. In minutes you will "turn that frown upside down." You will bring that person back to a great place. You will be SERVING THEM!

Try it. Go up to a person and practice what you learned in the last chapter, and watch how you serve them and bring them into a good space. Isn't this cool? We're multi-tasking our personality enhancement. This is AWESOME!

The greatest form of service to others is simple everyday courtesy. You don't be courteous. It's a choice— a powerful choice!

Don't be afraid to open a door for someone. If some sneezes, say, "Bless you." If there is only one cookie left on the plate, offer it to another person. These little simple courtesies go a long way— inside and out.

Random Acts of Kindness

On a recent business trip, the plane was grounded for mechanical difficulties. There were three people working as part of the ground crew for the national airline that I was flying. Over the course of nine hours, they were bombarded by the 200 people that were constantly being aggressive with them, blaming them for everything that was going on.

I could feel the intensity of that angry mom who wasn't going to get home in time for her child's birthday party and who chose to take that out on the airline employee behind the counter. Or that 23 year old just coming back from Cancun, Mexico, still tired from a week of partying and expressing her frustration. Or the profane man from the Midwest who couldn't think of anything more productive to do than to swear at the lady behind the counter.

By the end of the day, these women behind the counter were literally beaten down. It wasn't their fault that the plane broke down. And quite frankly, I'm happy that the pilot made the decision to keep us on the ground and potentially save our lives, but others didn't see it that way.

I could see that these three women were shattered by the end of that long day. Then around 9:00 p.m., I came up with an idea. I ran through the airport as the stores were closing until I found what I was looking for. I purchased a little package, ran back to these ladies behind the counter, but they were gone. I chased them down.

I searched the hallway until I found the women dragging themselves to the crew room. I didn't know their names... I pulled from behind my back three bouquets of beautiful summer flowers. I gave one to each of the women, and I said, "Ladies, I'm sorry for what you've gone through today. I truly want to thank you for everything you've done. I don't know your names, and you don't know mine, but I just want you to know that there are people out there that are grateful for all you're doing."

Why am I telling you this? What does this have to do with Network Marketing?

I'm sharing this story with you because things like this fill your heart with the power and the passion for people, and if you're willing to do little things every day, you'll be strengthening those serving muscles in your heart and adding immeasurably to your own life. Don't be afraid to compliment that new person you've just introduced to your business. Make people feel important. Why? Because they truly are!

The people in your business will become your best friends. They are your allies.

These are the people you want to spend the rest of your life with, so make sure that they know how valuable they are to you.

Do things every day to increase your own life— to increase the betterment of other people— and I guarantee you you'll have a strong, successful business for life.

Put Others First

You absolutely have to like people to be in this industry. You have to be willing to do things for others before you do them for yourself.

Now, make no mistake about it— your goal is to be successful. You're no good to anybody unless you're feeling and being successful yourself. But one of the ways to achieve the ultimate success is to focus on other people and serve them. There is nothing better in this world than making other people happy.

If I can give you one piece of advice that's more important than anything else I've shared in this book, it's this:

If you want to build a big business, and you want to do it right, you have to love people.

Go out there every day and serve others. Before you go to bed every night, hug your wife, kiss your kids and put a smile on somebody's face. Random acts of kindness are powerful. They're good for your heart. They're good for other people's hearts.

On my return flight from another business trip, I had a great conversation with a person from Atlantic Canada who was sitting next to me named Bernie. We had a wonderful time together. As we started talking, I asked him questions about himself. I sincerely wanted to know, because he seemed like a great guy.

He told me he was a guidance counselor and that he had spent most of his life empowering and teaching others to want more. He talked about goal setting— helping and encouraging individuals to reach for what they want, never saying no and never giving up.

I walked away with his phone number— a new friend in Atlantic Canada – and, of course, a new opportunity to introduce somebody to this business.

I just don't stop. Why? Because I love people! If you truly love people, you will never stop talking about your business.

Give a Few Hours of Every Week to a Good Cause

It really doesn't matter where you're at in your life, someone needs your assistance. If you really want to become a great servant to others, start today.

My family and I have decided to volunteer a couple of hours a week in our community. We've realized that in spite of our busy lives, social calendars, kids here and there, we need to give back to our community.

You can do the same thing. Look around your community. Find a good charitable cause that feels right in your heart, and get in there and serve. This will help you to meet new people. In the process, you'll create new friendships, and you know what will happen next— people will know you, like you, and trust you...

Inspired Actions

How to Start Serving Others

1. Serve others by increasing your gravitational pull.

2. Do not interrupt others.

3. Be respectful of others.

4. Engage in random acts of kindness, the simpler the better.

5. Decide to be a philanthropist, and realize that you will grow into one.

6. Take time for your family.

7. Give a few hours every week to a good cause.

12

Live in the Now

"Declare today that you are blessed with creativity, courage, talent, and abundance. You are blessed with a strong will, self-control, and self-discipline…. You are blessed with a compassionate heart and a positive outlook. Declare that everything you put your hand to is going to prosper and succeed. Declare it today and every day!"

JOEL OSTEEN

My journey really began to change when I started to understand and appreciate gratitude and find meaning in the small elements of life, not just in the huge goals and targets and results that I hoped to create.

Joel Osteen ends his best-selling book, *Becoming a Better You*, with the advice to be happy now, and he reminds us that this is a choice. On your journey to achieving big goals, it is an important choice to be happy and fully present to your life right *now*.

The Pitfalls of Multitasking

I've always had many, many things going on in my life at the same time. At one time when I was a police detective, I ran two different companies at the same time. I've always been involved in social groups with my kids and with my Network Marketing business and I've always enjoyed many different relationships with lots of different people. I'm cursed (and blessed) with the kind of mind that has a thousand things going on at the same time.

What I've realized, though, is that even though I'm able to multitask, it hasn't always served me, because as I've told you, whenever I was with somebody, I was never really *with* them.

Do yourself a favor and watch some videos of Mother Teresa and Mahatma Gandhi and notice how they interacted with people. You'll see that they were intensely centered on the people they were with. They paid full attention to what was being said. They really listened and they were able to process what they heard.

When you're with someone and you can't remember the details of the conversation, this is a clue that you're not living in the now. That's exactly what used to happen to me. But now when I'm with people, I literally and figuratively focus on the words they're saying, how they're expressing themselves, and what they're seeking to communicate to me.

What's Truly Important?

So many people focus on trying to get to that pot of gold, and then, when they get there, the pot is empty. The gold was actually right there in the individual experiences, the joys that they lived with people along the way— their family, their children, their business associates, etc.

There are many stories of people who go through life, working so hard to achieve some goal they thought was meaningful, only to realize that while they were busy achieving monetary rewards, their relationships, their health, and their spiritual life suffered.

In the end they found themselves empty and lost, even in the midst of financial wealth and career advancement.

How many marriages that have fallen apart because one of the spouses was driven to obtain and achieve and become more, more, more— all the while thinking they were creating a better life for their family? By the time they reached their goal, their family was gone.

The secret lies in enjoying the journey, each and every step and bump along the way, and not losing sight of what's truly important.

Every one of the inspirational leaders learned this lesson.

I've read many stories about Kennedy. In spite of how busy he was in running the country, he always took time for his young family, especially his son and daughter. Both John F. Kennedy Jr. and his older sister Caroline helped create the impression of an ideal family living in the White House. There are many photos showing Kennedy playing with his children, and his love for them has become a lasting part of his legacy.

At Pierre Trudeau's funeral, his son told the story of how his dad took time to create a special memory for him. When Trudeau's son was about six years old, he went on his first "official" trip— he went with his father and his grandfather to the North Pole. His son said that, for him, the best thing about the trip was spending lots of time with his dad, because normally the Prime Minister was always working.

They reached Alert, Canada's northernmost point. Trudeau's son began to be a little bored, because somehow his dad still had lots of work he was doing. But then one "frozen, windswept Arctic afternoon," Trudeau bundled his son up, put him in a jeep, and took him on a "special, top-secret mission." They drove slowly past many gray buildings, finally turning a corner and stopping in front of a red building. Trudeau's son jumped out of the jeep and ran towards the door, but he was told to look in the window instead.

As he peered into the frost-covered window, in the gloomy half-light, he could just make out a figure hunched over a cluttered worktable... he was wearing a red suit trimmed with white fur! Trudeau's son said, "And that's when I understood just how powerful and wonderful my father was."

Lessons from My Early Network Marketing Days

My daughter Laura was born one month before I joined my first Network Marketing company. I went nuts with my business right away. I was just enthralled by the potential I saw.

Two years into the journey was when it first hit me: I realized that I had pretty much missed most of my daughter's first two years of life.

I remember very few details about her at age one or two. It's sad. I know those years can never be relived.

Many of you reading this book know exactly what I'm talking about. This is truly one of the most painful parts of my life today.

I'm sitting in the Denver airport right now, editing this chapter. As I read this paragraph about missing my daughter's first two years, I burst into tears. I'm having a hard time seeing the keyboard right now.

I have been gone for 12 days. During those past dozen days, I have been in Philippines, Indonesia, Singapore, and Utah, and now eight days before Christmas I am finally on my way home. I cannot wait to hug Julie and the kids today!

I remember when we were getting ready to celebrate Laura's first birthday. I was so focused on building my Network business that I had decided to work in Calgary, Alberta for the month, prospecting and working with my reps in that area. I missed my daughter's birthday. It's one of the biggest regrets of my life.

Luckily, Laura doesn't remember that. But I do. I made a conscious effort to be more involved in my family after that. It's working.

There's a song called *Cat's in the Cradle* by Cat Stevens that conveys this very message— that looking back you realize all too late that you'd like to be able to do things differently.

One of my friends often cites this song when he speaks to a crowd. The words are chilling to me. Every time I hear that song I cry, thinking about my first couple years in Network Marketing and how I missed being involved in my kids' lives. It reminds me to stay grounded and present— with them and with myself.

Everyone that is building a business or any other kind of entrepreneurial endeavor ought to realize that the journey itself is the most important part of the process.

If you're going to be successful in life, if you're going to be a true Inspirational Leader, you have to design your life so that you create time for what is most important to you— your family.

Inspirational Leaders all achieve this, and they're busier than any of us, yet they accomplish more than most of us will ever hope to.

Many people who are attempting to build a Network Marketing business are extremely driven. They see the opportunity, they grab it with both hands, and they begin going for it to the exclusion of all else that's going on in their life. That creates a huge imbalance.

In my own life, after I quit my job as a cop I sacrificed everything during my first two years in Network Marketing. I blocked everything else out. I was blinded by my desire to be successful in this industry. The money that I was making just made it worse because I saw bigger and bigger numbers. I honestly can't tell you how much I regret this. If I could do it all over again, I would approach my business very differently right from the start.

Schedule Time for What Is Most Important

After realizing how much of my children's lives I had already missed, I decided to live by a schedule. On that schedule, I block out time for my family.

I live by an agenda, and it's right there: Four nights a week, dinner with the family. I have time in my planner allotted for my kids and for my wife. Friday night I shut the phone off and my wife and I enjoy some time together after the kids go to bed. Most of the time we just stay at home and talk. Once in a while we get a sitter and go out for dinner. Either way, it's our time together— **no matter what.**

I have to keep reminding myself every day that what's truly important is the here and now, because I'm such a hugely goal-driven person. With my newfound awareness, I take more vacations with my family on a regular basis than I ever did before, and guess what? My business hasn't suffered at all!

Your ability to stay organized and focused and to create time in your schedule for your family will be directly related to your success in Network Marketing.

I've known way too many people that wanted to be so successful in Network Marketing that they blocked out their family and friends, their husbands, their wives, their kids, everything. And that blind desire to be successful in Network Marketing destroyed their families.

Success in Network Marketing doesn't require this. It is as simple as having an agenda and jotting time slots into it every single week for your family. It's not about the *quantity* of time; what's important is the *quality*. It's making sure that you don't forget about what is most important to you.

Remember, you got started in Network Marketing to create a better life for your family. You have to design your life every day to include time for your family now. Otherwise when you do become successful, you'll have forgotten how to spend quality time with time, and you'll be disconnected with whom they have become.

Some people use this as an excuse. They procrastinate and use their families as the excuse to keep from producing. These individuals would do well to take a long, hard look in the mirror. They have never crossed over into action, and so they remain unsuccessful.

Eventually something might come along that will force them to get moving. Procrastinating creates a tremendous amount of guilt. If this is something you struggle with, you can expedite the process by just *deciding*. The sooner you choose action, the better off you are. (We'll be covering this in the next chapter.)

194

There are two sides to the pendulum:

- There's the person who's going too fast with their blinders on, so focused on that one goal that they miss everything else going on around them. That's not being present.

- Then there's the other person that's so distracted by everything else that's going on around them that they can't ever focus on their goal, and that's not being present either.

The Solution

The way to stay present to your life while you are building for the future is to make sure that your future goals are balanced within the context of your whole life.

You want to make sure you take time for yourself and your health. You don't want to neglect your family— the very ones you want to create a better life for. Block out on your agenda the times you have set aside to work your business, and then work with total focus during those times. Set aside time to be with your family, and be fully present to them during those blocks of time. Allow your family to be part of your enterprise— together you will enjoy the journey so much more!

Inspired Actions

How to Live in the Now

1. When you are with someone, be fully focused on them.

2. Concentrate on the conversation you are having; block out other thoughts and distractions.

3. Schedule time for what's really important.

4. Don't seek success at the expense of your family.

5. Balance your future goals within the context of your whole life.

6. Enjoy the journey.

13

Just Do It

"The world has the habit of making room for the man
whose actions show that he knows where he is going."

NAPOLEON HILL

Has there ever been a more successful advertising tagline than
Nike's "Just Do It"?

That tagline, created over 20 years ago, received a lukewarm
reception from Nike executives, who were at the time on the
losing side of the "Sneaker Wars" with Reebok. Today, the
eight-letter phrase is among the two or three slogans in all of
advertising history rated most memorable, and Nike has
become the world's largest sporting goods company.

Those three simple words, written by Portland advertising
whiz Dan Wieden in 1988, symbolize clarity and practicality.
The simple, powerful slogan moved beyond the world of
physical fitness to become synonymous with forward progress
and achievement— not just for athletes, but for anyone with a
vision. People wrote to Nike saying that "Just Do It" had
inspired them to leave abusive husbands and achieve heroic
personal feats.

Our word "slogan" comes from the 16th century Scottish Gaelic phrase *sluagh-ghairm*: A combination of *sluagh,* which means "army," and *gairm,* meaning "shout." A slogan is literally a *battle cry.*

I'm definitely a "Just Do It" kind of guy. I'm the type of person who, when I get a thought in my head, I just do it.

Anything that I've ever wanted to make happen, I just decided to make happen.

This is both a good quality and a bad quality. It's good because there are so many people out there that never take action. They have great ideas. They have a huge "Whys" and desires, but they never translate these into action. The downside for me is that, for the longest time I'd take action on *every* new idea that would come along, which ended up being a real detriment.

You can read a million books on personal development. You can read every single thing there is to read on *how* to do it and *why* to do it and *when* to do it.

But the bottom line comes down to you just taking one step... forward.

It's all and always about *you* taking *action*.

I can't tell you the amount of times I've heard people say that they can't do something. The word "can't" drives me absolutely insane. When somebody says, "I can't," what they're really saying is:

"I'm afraid" or "I'm scared."

What they really mean is:

"I don't like the feeling that I get when I try something I don't know how to do" or "I'm afraid that it will give me pain" or "I don't know what will happen if I can't succeed."

People are afraid of pain. I always use the analogy of somebody burning their hand.

If you burn your hand once, you're going to be very careful not to do it again. If you fail once, or some endeavor doesn't bring you the success you expected, you're naturally going to be gun-shy about ever attempting something like that again.

If you burn your hand, you have every right not to want to burn your hand again. But you do not have the right to say, "I can't" about something you've never attempted before. How do you know you can't until you've actually attempted it? It just doesn't make sense.

"I can't" is flat out irresponsible. It's a choice. You always have a choice. And when you say you can't what you're really saying is, "I choose not to."

This business is not complicated. It's a simple business. It's not easy. It takes a lot of work.

I've been through some of the worst pain in the world. I've made more mistakes than anybody I know. I've lost all my friends in the process. But I realized in the darkest hours of my journey that there were people out there that have been through a lot worse.

Look at the seven Inspirational Leaders and what they've been through. We all bleed the same way. We all breathe the same way. We all eat the same way. We're all human beings. We all have the same mind. And we all have the same potential to be successful. I look at Warren Buffett, Steve Jobs, and Bill Gates, and I think, "If they can have success, why can't I?"

Studying the seven Inspirational Leaders and identifying the traits that made them successful enabled me to realize my core task and keep focused on it.

One step forward, day after day, I'd take one trait and work on it. And then, the next day, I went to work on one of the other nine.

One step forward. Day after day.

You, too, instinctively know that if we all breathe, eat, and bleed basically the same way. And you know we must all have that same inherent ability to be successful.

Complacency Will Kill You

Earlier I talked about reading Joel Osteen's book, *Becoming a Better You*. Joel spent a lot of time talking about the hereditary link to one's current state of reality. His thoughts fit here with the idea of complacency – if you are stuck in a rut right now, it may be a lineage problem, an environmental problem, or even a experience problem. The bottom line is this:

You CAN change it.

If you are in a complacent place right now, that truly is *the worst place* to be.

You have to take action.

But be careful if you are stuck in complacency right now. It can be dangerous. If you decide to take action the first thing you have to do is make a choice.

You can take a left turn and head in the direction where I found myself at the beginning of this book.

Or you can turn right and start on your own journey to Inspirational Leadership.

Now that you have read this book, you really have no excuses.

**Decide to take action. Make that choice.
Focus on *Being the Change*, and get ready
for a life of prosperity and abundance.**

Your Roadmap to Success

Start by identifying your core task, which in Network Marketing is prospecting. Focus on it, and then work on the other nine techniques. This will be your roadmap to success.

In the end, nothing matters if you don't take action.

If you're not trying, you're dying.

The success you're looking for is not a magic door. It's not Pandora's box waiting for you to open it. It's about taking one step forward— big or small. One step. Just do it.

It's about trying different strategies and techniques. It's about practicing what you're doing.

Not worrying about the income.

Taking action toward the outcome.

Running as fast you can, always moving in the direction you want to go.

I hope that you decide to take action, to *Just Do It*. Remember what Gandhi said. That one simple phrase became the catalyst for me:

"You must be the change you wish to see in the world."

And absolutely...

"You must be the change you wish to see in YOUR world."

I attended a training in Baton Rouge, Louisiana recently. One of the leaders I was working with stood in front of the group and said, "The most important thing is the outcome."

A thought jumped into my mind as he said that.

Our business is not about the income; it's about the outcome.

The outcome is what you are really after. If your why is big enough, it will give you the motivation and courage to take action.

It's not about the income. It's about the outcome.

This is a very powerful statement.

Your ability to take action is tied to the reason you're doing this business. If your reason is big enough, you'll do it. It's like the story I mentioned earlier in the book about the woman who realizes her son is trapped under a car and just lifts that car up to free him.

A fourteen-year-old boy in Florida was despondent about not being big enough or strong enough to make the football team. Leaving practice early one day, he was walking home when he saw a car hit a pole and careen into a retention pond. The car began to sink, with an elderly driver trapped inside.

Along with two other men, the young boy dove into the pond and swam some 50 feet to the sinking vehicle. Together they pulled the man from the car and swam back to the bank with him.

The boy later said that as he was watching the car sink, his instincts and what he called "a higher power" took over and "I just jumped in." He concluded that God wanted him to walk home that day rather than call his mom for a ride.

The paramedics described the rescue as amazing, because the water was deep and full of snakes and alligators. This is just one of many examples of people coming to the aid of a stranger, with no thought for their own safety. In the moment, they had a big enough reason to risk life and limb, and they just did it.

Everybody has the ability to take action. Every single one of us has the ability to go to work and to make things happen for ourselves. Those that aren't making things happen just haven't identified a reason big enough yet to move them to take action.

Successful people in Network Marketing are those who have discovered a big enough reason, and they've allowed that reason to propel them into action.

It's that simple.

If you want to be successful, you have to get your mind off of the money. That's tough when so many of us are struggling with debt and financial pressure. This makes it even more important to have a strong why— a very clearly defined outcome.

All of us have areas that require improvement. Hopefully, you haven't been abandoned by all of your friends the way that I was, but that did cause me to examine who and how I was.

Next came a series of events in my life that caused me to study these Inspirational Leaders, and from that I saw the characteristics I wanted to develop in myself. I decided to focus on those characteristics and let the results just happen. And they did!

You're reading this book right now, so I know there's no reason you can't take my advice. You don't have to recreate the wheel. You can just follow what worked for me.

Once you get that core task perfected, focus on the other nine points.

- Become a better person.

- Work on developing your own gravitational pull.

- Realize that life is about serving other people.

- Pay more attention to details, build your confidence, and improve your communication skills.

All of these things work together.

And, of course, find a great mentor. Find somebody who has the success you want. Find somebody that has the same type of personality that you aspire to have, and be willing to trust that person enough to take their advice.

You'll become the inspirational leader that you want to be. But nothing will happen if you don't take action.

I didn't write this book in order to become an author and make a million dollars and go on a speaking tour. I wrote this book for a couple of very simple reasons:

As a public statement of what I'm choosing to be:

- Accountable for in my life, and

- To help find a cure for the disease that killed my dad.

I am committed to continuing on the road to success myself. I've read many books over the years that have assisted me to develop this mindset.

If you want to achieve the ultimate success you're looking for, then you must do what other leaders are doing. True leaders are always students; they're always reading; they're always developing.

At the back of this book, I've included a list of the books that have assisted me to make the profound personality changes I desired. Now that you have finished my book, recommend it to someone else and pick your next read from the list I've provided at the back.

I know that just like me, you, too, have the ability to be great. We are all born with the same unlimited potential. The difference between me and many other individuals is... I took action.

I guarantee you that whatever challenges you are facing today, whatever roadblocks or hurdles are in front of you, you can overcome them like I did. Please don't be a person that reads a book, puts it back on the shelf, and hopes and dreams about a better life. Take action on the changes you want to see in your life.

"Do the thing," Emerson said, "and you will have the power."

Just do it.

Are you willing to take action? To "Just do it?"

If you are, that's really Great! I want you to know you can count on my support and encouragement.

One more question...

When? When will you take action?

You know that I like to coin words and phrases as I did with "core task" and "gravitational pull." I'm not being arrogant when I do that thinking I know better. It's just that in my studies of these Inspirational Leaders I kept finding many powerful traits they *all* shared in common. One of those resonated with me immediately was their answer to the question, "When?"

It was always... NOW!

Right now. Not later. Not after this or that. Not "I'll think about it..." or "I need to know more." It was NOW.

I'm going to be bold enough to suggest an improvement on Nike's award winning slogan "Just Do It," to...

Just Do It... *NOW!*

So, when will you take action?

I hope there's only one answer for you. Just do it... NOW!

We're All in This Together

One person with passion can move mountains. The passion that you're developing by listening, learning, and growing will be the key to your success in this business.

Tell yourself today that you're going to take action and that you're not going to stop until your goals are accomplished. You and the thousands of people that are joining your opportunity are not wrong. Together, a team will be built, an empire will be created around you— thousands of people that are using the products and the services of your company— and with that you'll get everything you want out of your business.

You can make a difference.

You can BE the difference.

If you've never done this before, don't worry. Neither had I. We're all in this together.

I hope that my story has given you the courage and confidence to become an Inspirational Leader in your own world. If *I* was able to overcome the challenges I've shared with you in these pages, then nothing can stop *you* from overcoming whatever has been holding you back. I wish you much success and joy on your journey!

Recommended Reading

- *Becoming a Better You* by Joel Olsteen

- *Mach II with Your Hair on Fire* by Richard Brooke

- *How to Make People Like You in 90 Seconds or Less* by Nicholas Boothman

- *Where Have All the Leaders Gone?* By Lee Iacocca

- *The New Professionals: The Rise of Network Marketing as the Next Major Profession* by James W. Robinson

- *Your First Year in Network Marketing: Overcome Your Fears, Experience Success, and Achieve Your Dreams!* by Mark Yarnell and Rene Reid Yarnell

- *The Greatest Networker in the World* by John Milton Fogg

- *Good to Great: Why Some Companies Make the Leap... and Others Don't* by Jim Collins

- *How to Win Friends and Influence* People by Dale Carnegie

- *A Return to Love* by Marianne Williamson

- *Influencer: The Power to Change Anything* by Kerry Patterson, Joseph Grenny, David Maxfield and Ron McMillan

- *Snowball: Warren Buffett and the Business of Life* by Alice Schroeder

- *Think and Grow Rich* by Napoleon Hill

- *One Thousand Ways to Make $1,000 (Practical Suggestions, Based on Actual Experience, for Starting a Business of Your Own and Making Money in Your Spare Time)* by F. C. Minaker

- *Launching a Leadership Revolution* by Orrin Woodward

- *The Intelligent Investor: The Definitive Book on Value Investing. A Book of Practical Counsel (Revised Edition)* by Benjamin Graham, Jason Zweig and Warren E. Buffet by

- *The Most Important Minute* by Ken Dunn

- *Why Good Things Happen to Good People* by Stephen Post and Jill Neimark

Visit www.BeingTheChange.biz for these books as well as others from my personal reading list which updates regularly.

About the Author:

Ken is one of the leadership training world's up and coming great speakers and trainings. An incredible hunger to learn and teach others has lead Ken successfully through five different professional careers in the past 25 years.

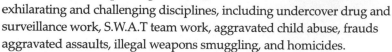

Ken began a policing career at the age of 18. He was involved in the policing world's most exhilarating and challenging disciplines, including undercover drug and surveillance work, S.W.A.T team work, aggravated child abuse, frauds aggravated assaults, illegal weapons smuggling, and homicides.

The birth of Ken's first child left him yearning for a career change. In the next ten years, Ken opened four different home businesses in four different industries (importing, property management, mortgage, and direct sales) and made millions of dollars from home in each profession.

In direct sales, Ken has assisted in building communities in excess of 250,000 people in over forty countries. Ken has helped dozens of families create new lives for themselves and significant seven figure incomes. As well, Ken has consulted with several direct sales company owners to successfully launch and scale their businesses around the world.

In 2008, Ken published his first book, *From Here to Having It All*, which attracted significant attention and sold thousands of copies. Jan 2010 brought Ken's second book, *The Most Important Minute*. Ken has also published a number of popular audio and video training sets, which are now commonly used as reference tools in the direct sales and mortgage industries. Ken is a living example that a sharp focus on leadership development and relationship building will yield success in any endeavor.

Today, Ken regularly speaks to groups in the I direct sales, mortgage, insurance, and banking industries. He uses humor and his own experiences to inspire audiences around the world.

Ken lives in Toronto, Canada with his wife Julie, and children Matthew and Laura.

www.facebook.com/kendunnleadership

Publishing and Ordering Information

Being The Change
Inspired to Win In Network Marketing
by KEN DUNN

Available online at:
www.evolvlifepublishing.com
www.amazon.com
www.beingthechange.biz

Contact the Publisher for Bulk order Discounts

For more information about bulk purchasing,
or affiliate marketing sales contact
EvolvLife Publishing directly at:
1-905-477-1219 or
info@evolvlifepublishing.com.

EvolvLife Publishing
1305 Morningside Drive, Unit 15
Scarborough, Ontario, Canada

www.kendunnleadership.com

www.kendunnleadership.com

Check in with Ken regularly and read his latest entries on leadership and life. Ken has developed a reputation globally for his tenacious study of all things leadership. He believes that all success in life starts with developing an ability to lead. The blog chronicles his studies, with a sharp focus on leading one's self. If you have ever had a true desire to become a better leader, start here!

The Most Important Minute In Your Network Marketing Career

In *The Most Important Minute* Ken will show you that there really is One Minute in your Network Marketing Career that is more important than any other period of time. Understanding the Most Important Minute, and what to do with it, will save you years of pain and learning in network marketing.

What others are saying:

"One of the best books that I have ever read about network marketing and starting a business properly. I bought 1000 copies for my entire company." ~ Orjan Saele, MLM Owner and Million Dollar Income Earning Distributor, Norway

"A Great Read for anyone in Network Marketing" ~ Art Jonak, MLM Rock Star, www.artjonak.com

"I have watched Ken learn the business over the years. He is truly a master networker. This book is truly a small example of the understanding that he has. This book has to be read by anyone in network marketing." ~ Juan Carlos Barrios, Million Dollar Earner, Mexico

"In my 17 in the Network Marketing Profession, I have never understood the roadmap to success in our business as well as I do after reading the *Most Important Minute*. Ken's teachings are revolutionary. A must read for anyone, old or new, to our business." ~ Mike Healy, Million Dollar Earner, USA